BORN FOR THE WILD COUNTRY

BIG FEET AND A MOUTH TO MATCH

CHILCO
CHOATE

Heritage House

CANADIAN CATALOGUING IN PUBLICATION DATA

Choate, Chilco, 1935-
Born for the wild country

ISBN 1-895811-59-7

1. Choate, Chilco, 1935-
2. Chilcotin River Region (B.C.)—Biography
I. Title

FC3845.C445Z49 1998 971.1'7504'092 C98-910127-4
F1089.C445C55 1998

First Edition 1998

Heritage House wishes to acknowledge the support of Heritage Canada, the British Columbia Arts Council, and the Cultural Services Branch of the Ministry of Small Business, Tourism and Culture.

Heritage House Publishing Company Ltd.
Unit #8 – 17921 55th Ave., Surrey, BC V3S 6C4

Cover design: Darlene Nickull
Book design and typesetting: Darlene Nickull
Cover photos: Chilco Choate
Edited by: Audrey McClellan

Printed in Canada

DEDICATION

To the Hasler brothers, Tom, Harry, and Almont, who taught the lessons, and especially to my parents, Fred and Avis Choate, without whose mental endurance the kid would probably have ended up becoming a cog in someone else's wheel.

Cheers from the Chilcotin,

CONTENTS

FOREWORD

The "Bionic Man" of B.C.'s Cariboo/Chilcotin is sticking closer to home these days. Chilco Choate is about as deaf as a stone even with his twin hearing aids cranked up to full volume, and he's stopped going to public hearings he can't hear—good news for the loggers, ranchers, and two-bit politicians he used to harass. Assisted by his solar-powered computer and fax machine and inspired more by utter boredom than the success of his first book, *Unfriendly Neighbours*, he has finally produced his second.

Born for the Wild Country: Big Feet and a Mouth to Match, is about Choate's many adventures growing up in White Rock, escaping the clutches of parents, teachers, and school principals in favour of days spent along the shores of the Nicomekl River when frogs were as big as chickens. A six-foot twelve year old with size thirteen feet was about as good a fit with a school desk as Choate would be with the urban world that was closing in around him. So-called civilization and Choate could never mix without dire consequences. He remains in self-imposed exile to this day, much to the relief of everyone that knows him, still a reasonably safe distance from the rest of the world, where he keeps his own perspective on life and writes about the boy who got away.

John Taylor
Telefilm Canada
1998

CHAPTER I

SOUTHPAW

We all know our own case best and in my case I have spent a lifetime trying to figure out why and how I am where and what I am. Well now, by God, all that figuring has finally paid off because just a few nights ago I awoke with a crystal clear memory. As it turns out, my situation in this world is not my fault. Instead, just as I always hoped, it is somebody else's fault. Now let me tell you an honest to God fact, partner. That happens to be about the most comfortable enlightenment that a person can wake up to.

In this case the problem began a long time ago—in 1941 to be exact. Don't jump to the conclusion that I'm blaming Hitler, because he had nothing to do with it. Neither did the war he started. But the problem did develop around a powerful-minded person and in a specific place. That place happened to be a concentration camp-style building in the small coastal town of White Rock, British Columbia, which bore the name of White Rock Elementary. At that time, the fresh inductees into Grade 1 had a small building set off to one side for them. Some privilege. It was not the four walls of the building that created its ominous atmosphere (although they certainly helped), but the presence of the commandant on the inside who went under the disguise of a teacher. She had the name Miss Something-or-Other. I cannot recall what it was, even though as I sit here writing these words over fifty years later, her face still comes to me just as plain as if she were standing right at my elbow, waiting and daring me to stumble over some little irregularity. She was good at that. God, was she ever. She was big (bigger than me), old (maybe 20 or more), wore glasses (we called her Old Four Eyes), and if memory serves me right, she almost always wore a red dress. She possessed all the trappings of a commandant, being legally delegated with the rank, authority, and weapons to do what she considered to be the job. She wielded the wooden pointer that she carried at all times like a camp guard did his gun. And let me tell you, she knew how to use it too.

It's doubtful if fifty-year-old memories are perfect, but they are accurate enough to remember the critical events we are about to get into here. And I think it's safe for me to say the following episode occurred not long after my first day at school.

Now you can believe this or not, but when I was six years old I was shy and quiet, I sometimes stuttered, and I was VERY obedient. As my mother told me on many occasions, "Teddy, you are the best little boy I have ever raised." How could any kid expect to do better than that?

Then there came that fateful day in 1941 when the earth opened up, the Devil roared, and the sky fell. Life was never to be the same again. There I was, sitting at my desk drawing or writing or trying to do whatever it was that Old Four Eyes had told us to do. I had already noted that this teacher had the ability to prowl (it was not a walk) up and down the aisles of the room as quietly and stealthily as a hungry cat patrols its own barn. Even at the age of six I was aware of such things and could sense that this was the trait of a true hunter, a quality I appreciated. This woman projected the image of a successful hunter and those are the only kind that count, so Old Four Eyes and I shared some mutual values. At least I figured we did until that day she revealed her true colours and all hell proceeded to cut loose.

Old Four Eyes had come up behind me and I sensed she was interested in what I was doing, so I began putting total effort into whatever it was. Then right out of the clear blue, WHACK! With that pointer she knocked the pencil out of my hand and it flew into the next aisle. The next moment she was tapping me on top of my head with the pointer as she asked in the hardest voice I had ever heard, "Who taught you to hold a pencil in your left hand?"

I had no idea what she was talking about. For one thing, I doubt we had been taught yet about the difference between left and right. Can you remember situations like that when you were six? In my own case, when I slip back in time my body still tenses a bit whenever these thoughts resurface. That sandy feeling in my mouth comes back too. And another thing I noticed then and remember to this day was that every other kid in that room was staring directly at me.

"Has the cat got your tongue?" the teacher demanded to know.

I had been taught at home about cats and tongues so whispered back, "No."

"Well then answer me," she further demanded.

What does a six-year-old kid say or do under circumstances like that? My mind was both spinning and frozen if such a thing is possible, and I could not remember who had taught me to use a pencil. It was probably one of my older sisters, but by then I was afraid to say so for fear that this terrible wrath might descend onto them too. I sort of liked my sisters and did not want to get them involved in whatever was beginning to happen.

Old Four Eyes had moved forward and was now standing right in front of me with hands on hips, glaring as only a Grade 1 teacher knows how to do. She was obviously waiting for my reply.

I had never been taught to pray, but every living creature is born with that natural built-in escape valve and my overwhelming prayer was that Dad would come bursting through the school door and relieve this impossible situation. It didn't happen.

After a few breathless moments I was able to make my numb mind come up with an answer that I hoped would fend off this assault. I remembered what my Dad had mentioned on several occasions, "Teddy seems to be left-handed. Some day he is going to become a famous baseball pitcher just like his Dad used to be." (When Dad was young he actually did pitch for the early Capilano baseball team in Vancouver, and there is a picture of him there in a sports gallery.) When Dad said things like this it left an impression in my mind that whatever I was doing was the right thing. It made me feel good knowing that I was able to do things that my sisters, for some reason, were not able to do. Neither Mom nor Dad ever told my sisters that they were scheduled to be famous baseball players some day and that did set my mind to wondering just why and what it was that was making me different.

The teacher was becoming impatient because she was shifting the pointer around. It appeared she was going to speak again. I beat her to the word. "My Dad says I'm supposed to pitch baseball," I stammered in a whisper.

"Oh he did, did he?" Old Four Eyes replied. "And what pray tell me did he tell you to do at school?"

I could not remember anything in particular that Dad had told me to do in school other than to be sure and do everything the teacher told me to do. My natural response and hopeful protection was, "I don't know."

"Well, if you don't know, then I'm going to find out," she informed me as she absent-mindedly tapped the edge of the desk with the pointer. "Before you leave school today, you come up to my desk because I'm sending a note home with you to your parents."

WOW. Things were going from impossible to worse. I already knew from listening to my sisters that a note to home from school meant bad trouble, like very quiet dinners with orders to "sit right up there and clean everything off your plate, even the boiled onions." Now, half a century later, there is still not the slightest question that that teacher had me in a "state." As I sit here rediscovering the memories of those days, I get a feeling of total frustration again. Old Four Eyes must have had a powerful personality.

The teacher was still standing there staring at me. She appeared to be in deep thought and I can remember beginning to hope that the danger was past. The rest of the class must also have sensed it was over because a girl in the next aisle reached down and retrieved my pencil, which she then laid in the trough on my desk. That seemed to bring Old Four Eyes back to a somewhat more normal disposition, as she nodded to the pencil and instructed me, "You are going to learn to use your *right* hand and you are going to begin doing it *right* now." She pointed to the pencil with her pointer as she said, "Let me see you pick up that pencil with your *right* hand and start drawing with it."

I was afraid to ask her what she wanted me to draw, but I had already been told that I was a good drawer, so the confidence I had left told me I now had a chance to redeem myself. Anything to relieve the tension of the situation. I picked up the pencil and just as I was about to mark something onto the paper, WHACK! She laid that pointer right across my wrist. Once again the pencil went flying, but this time that wasn't enough to appease her as she reached down and grabbed me by the hair and used it to jerk me right out into the aisle.

"What did I just tell you?" she screamed. I became speechless and started to cry. At that point she shifted her hold onto my shoulder and used it to drive me back down into the seat again as she continued screaming, "Don't you ever let me catch you picking up a pencil with your left hand again."

At that remark I broke out into a real barn-rattling bellow. Crying turned out to be no defence against someone like her. This time she grabbed me by the shirt collar and used it to jerk me back into the aisle. She spun me around to face the back of the room and gave a shove in that direction. "If you are going to make that kind of racket, then just go out into the cloakroom until you quieten down. After that you can come back in and do your work properly."

As soon as I got into the cloakroom and closed the door between us, I felt relief. I can still remember sitting there crying my eyes out until there were no tears to come. Several times that day the teacher came to the door and asked if I was ready to go back in and rejoin the class again, but the only answer she ever received was a silent headshake. There was a seat in the cloakroom from which I could see out into the trees and bushland that came down close to the schoolyard, and the sight and feel of the green quietness had a profound and warm effect on me. Oh to be as free as a fox or a deer.

Even though my parents did intervene on my behalf, this southpaw problem continued throughout that first year at school. Old Four Eyes never did let up on me much. She must have been a spiteful person because even after making some sort of agreement to concede to my "problem," it still seemed to bother her so much that she would sometimes go into a rage when watching me work or print left-handed. When she blew up that way, she often broke one of those pointers over my head, neck, or shoulders. And I can still see her standing beside her desk and throwing chalk at me. Luckily she was no great shakes as a pitcher and she seldom threw good strikes, but there were a few times when she made good hits on some of the other kids. It happened often enough that only the bravest wanted to sit near me.

After all of these years I do know for sure that Old Four Eyes was the one most responsible for launching me into my life's course, even though it was probably not intentional. It's hard to tell if her cooling-off-in-the-cloakroom system was as much a relief for her as it was for me, but that is exactly what it became—a relief valve. The first time she broke one of those pointers because of me was shortly after she had agreed to get off my back. On this particular day I was maybe not being as watchful as I should have been. Old Four Eyes was on the prowl and before I realized it she was behind me and within striking distance. I could not lay my pencil down or fake using my right hand, which I had learned to do. Out of the corner of my eye I saw the roundhouse swing coming. Given my predicament, my reflexes were continuously improving and this time mine were faster than hers. Before the pointer hit its intended target, I jerked my arm back so that she missed both the hand and the pencil. She did, however, smash the desk with a good enough crack that pointer splinters went flying all over the room.

This brought her up into a real rage and she screamed at me, "For that little trick I'm sending a note home to your father and he is going to have to pay the school sixty cents to replace the pointer that you are responsible for breaking."

This information came as very bad news because I could see that money coming out of my own piggy bank. Old Four Eyes was true to her word. She did write the note and I did deliver it home as instructed. The system was not unlike the old Roman practice of making the vanquished carry crosses to their own crucifixions. But in this case I do not believe the teacher received her satisfaction. As far as I know, Dad never paid such a bill and I know that no payment was ever asked for from me.

My life's course was set just a few weeks later when a similar episode occurred and I was sent to that familiar cloakroom. This time I simply picked my coat off the wall hanger and kept right on going straight through the outside door into the nearby bushland. In those days there was still scrub bushland in the three miles between the school and our home. It was there, sheltered from the woman with the stick, that I felt comfort and security. There is no doubt in my own mind that was the day I discovered my true and natural calling.

That was my first "hooky" day, and it ended with mixed feelings on my part. As soon as I got clear of the school and knew that nobody was coming after me, I put my mind into devious gear. Normally we Choate kids travelled the three miles to school in a schoolbus, but I decided that rather than return to the schoolyard to catch the bus in the afternoon, I would just walk parallel to the road all the way home and wait for the bus to arrive at its stopping place. Then I would accompany my sisters to the house. However, things didn't work out quite that way. There must have been too many things to do or check out along that walk because even with my head start, the bus got home before I did. That meant my sisters arrived home before me and all they could tell Mom and Dad was nobody knew where I had headed. When I walked through the door an hour or so late, Mom and Dad already had their coats on and were getting ready to come look for me. They didn't show any noticeable relief when they began grilling me instead.

There was a painful price paid for that day's freedom, but as time went on it became a price that I was prepared to pay with less and less provocation. If there was any victory won it fell to me, because within a year all of the administrators had given up on me and I could pretty much set my own school days as I pleased. Fifty years later I can conclude that Old Four Eyes did me a favour of sorts.

But just the same, that year of 1941 was a long time passing. The "instruction" mentioned here was only part of how "They" tried to make us do what "They" deemed to be right. For instance, I recall being made to sit all day with my left hand folded behind my back while Old Four Eyes stood behind me with a wooden ruler or pointer poised for action. She could be mighty handy with a yardstick too. I can still remember Old Four Eyes' apparent enthusiasm when she had to deal with one of her Grade 1 burdens. Because of that I have never forgotten that bitch and I will never forgive her either.

There are probably people who think these ramblings are just part of old Choate's campfire stories, which they sort of are. At the same time, they are based on absolute truth. Since those days I've met several other southpaws of my own vintage, and most of them have commented that I got off no better or worse than they did. I also met a person who was actually a teacher from that time and he laughingly told me, "God, you were one of the luckier ones. Some teachers went so far overboard with those ideas that they actually tied a kid's left hand behind his back and would leave him that way all day long. And do you want to know something else about that?" he continued, laughing. "Some of those kids even ended up becoming right-handed, just like the rest of us." This fellow was referring to a different school and province, so anti-left-handedness must have been pretty much the norm at that time.

I'm not sure when this part of the educational system was officially changed, but during that year of 1941 I hookied out of so much school that they failed me and I had to repeat Grade 1 in 1942. By that year either the system had changed or the new teacher refused to enforce it, because at White Rock Elementary there was no more fuss about which hand I used.

So that was one of the ways that "They" used to make us bend to the stuffed shirts of authority. When I think back, it was similar to beating "the fear of God" into a kid. Within some families, that was still common in the 1940s. Luckily times change. Or do they?

Writing this story has just jogged another memory, this one from more recent times. It would have been about fifteen years later, when I was grown up and working with a man named Slippery Slick. At an earlier time he had been a teacher of sorts. Slick had spent World War Two as a "close combat" instructor for U.S. paratroopers and had even risen to the rank of First Lieutenant. On this particular day the southpaw subject had arisen again in the form of a broadaxe that had a moulded right-hand handle fitted into it. (Broadaxes have a deliberate curve in their handles and blades so they must be used as either left- or right-handed but not both ways. I have never seen one made for a lefty.) I was working up on the wall of a log cabin that we were building, hewing the inside of a log and doing it right-handed, which made for slow and clumsy progress. Slick was sitting on a block of wood down on the ground and had been watching me struggle with the job until he couldn't hold himself in any longer. He then informed me in his southern Arkansas drawl, "Slim, you ain't left-handed. You is WRONG-handed."

CHAPTER 2

SKUNKS

Do you like skunks? The kind that people trip over while on their last trip to the House of Lords in the dark at night? You know the ones I mean—"Bush Pussies." Well, by golly, I like them too and my affection goes back quite a way, to 1943 or 1944 to be exact, when I would have been eight or nine years old.

It all began by accident as a spin-off from my newest financial enterprise that was going to make me rich—this time it was trapping. I came to have an interest in trapping after an old man from the Peace River country retired to the southern climes of Surrey and bought the farm next to ours. This was in the small farming community called Elgin, or sometimes Port Elgin, which is spread out along the flood plains of the Nicomekl and Serpentine Rivers, which in turn are about three miles north of White Rock. Some of the hill area between White Rock, Crescent Beach, and the Nicomekl was considered to be part of Elgin too. There were no actual boundaries to the community, so people who lived anywhere in the general area could declare themselves in or out of Elgin as there was no way to challenge those decisions.

At that time there were no stores in Elgin and only two buildings had signs identifying them as part of the community. One of these was the one-room school located on a hill up in the bush. The wheel tracks that went past it were called the Semiahmoo Trail, which was originally an old Indian trail that led from somewhere near the lower Fraser River to all points south. The other named building was the Elgin Community Hall, located beside the only paved road in the area—the road to Crescent Beach. The King George Highway was still being built.

I believe the centre of the community, at least from the kids' point of view, was the concrete bridge structure that contained the floodgates on the Nicomekl River. This was the best swimming hole in the area, so it became the major gathering place. It was also a pretty good spot to fish when the sea trout and cutthroats were running.

The only commercial businesses I can remember were the gas pump operated by the Lowney family and, almost across the road from it, Bill Hadden's blacksmith and boat operation. They were just a short gunshot from the Elgin Bridge, or The Dam as it was often referred to. Other than the farms, that was pretty much what Elgin consisted of during the early 1940s. At that time the farming along the flood plain was mixed—dairy, potatoes, oats, hay, and mixed vegetables—and was very productive. Then there were the other farms up on the hill, like the one we had, that were not nearly as productive and were often referred to as "stump farms." It was a pretty accurate description too. The farmers on these upper acreages were growing things like berries, goats, rabbits, and lots of those hard stumps. I can still remember my Dad commenting that the stumps always seemed to outnumber anything else we tried raising, but he was at a loss trying to figure out a way to make any money from them.

Aside from stumps there was one other crop the hillside farms produced more of than the rich ones down on the bottomland did, and that was kids. I do not remember why that was, but I do remember both Mom and Dad referring to this phenomenon and they did not consider it to be a commercial asset for the hill people. At school we were sometimes referred to as "bushrats" or just "bushies." And we in turn referred to the kids from the lower farms as "river-rats." Our farm was quite close to the river, so we Choate kids were able to relate both ways depending on who we were associating with at the time.

The major difference between our family and the new Peace River man, whose farm was both upper and lower, was that Tom Hasler was RICH. He was rich in more ways than with money too. Tom owned and packed guns everywhere he went, even though the largest wild animals that lived in the area were Columbia blacktail deer and foxes. There was also the rare report when somebody claimed to have seen a cougar, but as Dad used to say, he would believe it when he saw a hide nailed to a wall. There were several species of smaller animals like rabbits, mink, an occasional bobcat, muskrats, the odd raccoon, and of course quite a few of those little stinkers that some of this story is about.

I can remember the word "crooks" being used, but in those days they all lived in the City of Vancouver, which was thirty miles away, or between the pages of comic books that cost ten cents each. So there was no particular reason for a person living in Surrey to feel that he had to be perpetually armed, but this man from the north had lived in a different world to ours and he often told me he refused to trust any animal that walked on two legs. Tom Hasler was neither big nor impressive-looking, and he must have been in his late sixties, but to an eight-year-old country kid at Elgin, this guy walked as tall in the saddle as any man could. Other kids had heroes in the movies and comic books, but I had a real live one who lived right next door. Over the following few years I was able to keep him pretty much to myself too, as I cannot remember any other kid getting past Tom's front door.

When Tom Hasler bought this sixty-acre farm in 1943, the only habitable building on it was a clapboard shack affair with an almost flat roof that Dad had built for the previous owner, J.A. Borthwick. The first time I met Tom must have been just a day or two after he had moved in. He was sitting on a stump in front of his new home, surveying his domain. We introduced ourselves and he then made room on the stump and invited me to share it with him while we "chewed the fat" for a while. He apparently had no friends or acquaintances in the immediate area nor knew anything about his new neighbours, so I was delighted to be able to tell him all I knew about everybody and everything. Tom was real appreciative of my information and in return he began talking to me straight on, as two adults would do. Tom never talked down to me, so all of a sudden I felt that I had grown a foot or more. We also discovered that we had mutual interests. I knew this for sure when I saw a whole bunch of guns stacked in a corner and hanging from spikes on the walls of the house. Tom took them down one by one and let me handle them as he showed me how they worked.

It was a warm afternoon, so we retired back out to the stump. After we got resettled, Tom nodded towards his new home and asked me, "Do you know who built that shack?"

Of course I knew because I had even helped Dad when he did it, so I proudly replied, "Dad and I built it for Mr. Borthwick." I could remember Mr. Borthwick referring to the place as his "cabin," which I thought made it sound real woodsy, so I relayed this to Tom also.

Tom began to chuckle and nodded towards the cabin again as he informed me, "Where I come from, if you tried to winter in a place like that you would freeze to death the very first night. That building ain't no cabin because a real cabin is made of logs and has a better roof. Why this goddam thing is nothing but a shack." He then thoughtfully remarked, "If I can locate enough trees of the right size around here, I think I'll build me one last cabin."

"Can I help you build it?" I asked excitedly.

"Sure you can," Tom promised, "because I'm not as limber as I used to be and I'll bet you can jump around on a cabin wall better than a squirrel. There's lots of up and down work to building a log cabin and it takes somebody with a lot of energy and know-how, so if you supply the energy, I'll supply the know-how and between us we'll have a cabin up in no time. But we have to locate the right trees and get them over here first, so we'll go look for them as soon as I get better settled in."

Talk about lucky breaks. What other kid could even dream of having a neighbour like this man? We spent most of the rest of the afternoon sitting on the stump as we chewed the fat. That's when Tom began telling me all about where he had come from and all the interesting things he had done up in the north country, like hunting for moose, caribou, bear, and all sorts of other things. By evening suppertime I was all a-tremble with excitement and could hardly wait to tell my family about our new and wonderful neighbour who had befriended me.

As it turned out, for reasons I no longer remember we never did get started on building Tom a new cabin. Possibly we did not find enough trees of the size Tom figured would be needed, so at some later day the plan was officially put to rest and Tom and I resigned ourselves to his living in what became known as "Old Tom's Shack." And for the next three years the most exciting stories and plans that any kid has ever listened to or been allowed to partake in poured out of that shack. They were not just stories for starry-eyed kids either, because after Tom got to know some of his adult neighbours, he could spellbind them also. The stories he told the adults were mostly about how he had spent the Depression years trapping all over the north country and how some of those years he and one of his brothers came out of the bush with $25,000 worth of furs. Tom told my family these stories in the mid-1940s, when Dad was lucky if he found an outside job that paid as much as a dollar an hour. Those jobs were considered an improvement over the pre-war and early war years when he had worked as a sharecropper on the same farm that Tom now owned.

Even I found the money stories fascinating as at eight years of age I was becoming aware of the value of money and the difficulty of acquiring it. Country kids seldom received "allowances," as city kids did. We were expected to work for our "dole," so didn't get any money for chores we did around our own home and had to find paying work with somebody else, which wasn't easy to do. So far the acquisition was not happening as fast as my appetite for things like ice cream and pop could eat it up. Like most country people, we considered Eaton's catalogue to be the family bible and the things in there—like a factory-made fishing reel and a hunting knife that was needed in the worst way—cost more than I had been able to save up. When Dad had sharecropped for Mr. Borthwick, they set me up with my first money job, but it was of a type that never really caught my liking. I was five or six years old, and it did not take a young mind long to realize that picking spuds for ten cents a sack was a slow and dull way to become rich. Those were 100-pound sacks too, and the farmers set up scales out in the fields to weigh them with. And do you know, some of those farmers were so mean-spirited that they demanded at least 110 pounds in the sacks. They claimed this was to make up for the clods of good black earth that some kids would drop in with the spuds to make a nice rounded-looking sack. (I learned never to put the clods in the bottom of the sack as they could be seen leaking out. The best place was about in the middle.) The farmers argued this extra weight requirement made for a fair system, but at the same time, adult farm workers were being paid fifteen cents for a 100-pound sack (and not 110 pounds). As the kids were told time and again, an adult would never cheat like we might. Oh sure they wouldn't. The word "discrimination" was not in general use then, but there were young people growing up who had a gut feeling that something like it existed.

Besides my growing awareness of money, something else happened back about 1940 that certainly has a bearing on this story. Several of the neighbours began commenting on a strange transformation that was taking place in little Teddy Choate. Apparently he had developed an addiction, and the euphoric compound that had hooked him was the smell of burnt gunpowder. The sight and feel of the instruments that created the odour were beginning to have a profound effect on him too. And then there was the smell of burnt dynamite. This seemed to drive him into ecstasy, and his father, who sometimes worked as a powderman blowing stumps for other farmers, had to keep a watchful eye on his kid because Teddy had a dangerous habit of running up to the blasted holes to inhale the full aroma of the smoke before the wind blew it away. The danger came from the black powder fuse that was used in those days. It had a deadly habit of sometimes creating delayed firings, and when several charges were lit at the same time, the powderman had to keep track of how many explosions had actually gone off. Sometimes those sputtering delays fired several minutes late and on rare occasions they blew hours later.

The kid's addiction to this stuff was not necessarily considered a social problem in 1940, and in some ways it was viewed as an asset. Boys not much older than me were considered to be cannon fodder for the present war. Before 1939 the Allies had conned themselves into believing there would not be another major war and had been caught with their pants down. By 1940 their innocence was cured and people were saying that from then on they would believe what they sang in the Canadian anthem: "We stand on guard for thee." At public gatherings where this was sung, people would just bellow that line out. And as far back as I can remember, adults were telling us kids, "There will always be another war." With some people it was almost like a slogan. So we were being prepared both physically and mentally, and it was contagious and addictive. If you do not believe that's the way it was in Canada in those days, I'll jog your memory a bit further.

My parents were considered to be liberal thinkers, but even so, my last Christmas gift from Santa Claus was a new single-shot BB gun complete with two tubes of BB's. There was also a fine array of war toys and I am sure that they all had meaning for my expected future. Would you give a five-year-old boy an air gun with a box of shot and then turn him loose with it today? This makes for interesting contemplation as even though we were living in a violent world, there was very little street violence locally. That does make a person wonder a bit.

But to get back to the story, Tom Hasler and I hit it off real well together and that was lucky for me, though I still don't know exactly what it may have done for Tom. Perhaps because he never had any kids of his own (at least none that I ever heard of), he was willing to help put the finishing touches on somebody else's. If that was the case, then he sure as hell did a successful job on this one and I do appreciate the time and effort he gave it.

Old Tom's Shack was less than a five-minute run from our house, which meant that when Tom and I were not careful enough we could sometimes hear my mother hollering things like, "Teddy, WATER!" This meant that I was expected to go home immediately and carry several buckets of the stuff up the hill from the creek. (At the time, the creek that ran through our properties still had no name, but I suspect it must have one by today.) A strange thing about that trail between our homes was there seemed to be mental traffic lights on it. The run from our house over to Tom's took five minutes, but the walk back always took longer.

Another of Mom's yodels that created mixed feelings was, "Teddy, SUPPER!" If it was a day when I had been lucky enough to catch one of our half-wild Leghorn roosters that lived most of the time in the bush with the pheasants, then that could result in a faster homeward movement. But if there was no chicken for the pot, we were doomed to a veggie dinner, which was something worth avoiding. How are you with boiled onions? It's the same with me too, and it always has been. Mom insisted on calling them "creamed" onions, but the words did not alter the flavour one iota and they still resembled a plate of slimy slugs. Probably tasted about the same too. There was only one thing worse than those onions and that was parsnips, and unfortunately our garden was able to produce far too many of both. There were even times we were unlucky enough to have both of those poisons on the table at once. That would result in the slowest meal imaginable. Downright sickening is what those dinners were.

But Tom Hasler was a very wise man and so were his two brothers, Almont and Harry, who spent a lot of time at The Shack with us. Harry actually ended up living there most of the time, but Almont commuted back and forth from his own home over at Newton, about ten miles away. One of the first things I learned from these Peace River men was they really knew how to live right. I was often invited to join them at mealtimes, and it didn't matter if I had just eaten at home—the meals at The Shack were good enough that I never refused the bushmen's offer. There was always meat of some sort on their table, whether we killed it on the q.t. ourselves or they bought it from the butcher shop over at Cloverdale, seven miles away. The stores at White Rock, Crescent Beach, and Sunnyside were closer by half, but only Cloverdale had a liquor store and this crew understood its priorities.

When I say they knew how to live right, I really mean it. Sometimes their entire meal was simply meat, usually flavoured with big jolts of ketchup. These meals were not fancy ones by any means, as they were often just bacon and eggs, but don't think for a minute that these fellows didn't have the trailman's know-how to do things up right. You can make a mighty meal for four men when the cook is not chintzy, and none of the Haslers were. In the case of our bacon and egg menu, our usual fare worked out to be a dozen eggs and at least half a slab of bacon. For a breakfast or midday treat they would make up a mess of scrambled eggs that took an even two dozen, and into that concoction went a spoonful of every spice on the shelf.

Another thing they always had on the table was "baker's" bread, which at our house was a rare sight. Once in a while Tom would make us up a bannock in the black cast-iron Dutch oven and into it went an array of ingredients that most other people never had such as raisins, currants, and other hard-to-come-by fruits. Compared to the baking powder biscuits we had at home, those bannocks were out of sight. Even though there was food rationing, it never seemed to affect The Shack like it did other houses in the area. From some of the conversations at the table I learned that we were somehow different and it had a lot to do with Tom's money and Almont and Harry's "connections." Nobody ever explained the meaning of this to me other than by chuckling. One time I asked the crew some questions about it and I can still see Almont sitting there with his chair tipped back against the wall, smoking his pipe as he quietly shook his head and commented about those "other people," who he described as "Those poor dumb bastards." The rest of us just nodded in agreement. You can be assured that no parent or schoolteacher ever described a better way of life than the one we enjoyed at Old Tom's Shack.

There was something else that the Hasler boys always had on the table or in their pockets. They each had what seemed like a perpetual bottle of gin, made locally by United Distilleries Limited of Vancouver. At The Shack we referred to the stuff simply as the UDL. Of all the interesting things in The Shack, the booze was the only thing that was off limits for me. It was never offered, which was no problem because it was never asked for either. One of the reasons I never desired it was that the UDL had an aroma so strong it could stop a skunk dead in its tracks at a hundred feet. My Dad often talked about it that way too, so there was never a danger of this kid snitching so much as a swig. These were war years, and all liquor was rationed except this UDL gin. I can still remember my Dad telling us the reason it never had to be rationed was because it was such a bad brew that nobody but a drunken American sailor would try to drink it. He probably knew what he was talking about, because the major shareholder of UDL happened to be one of his cousins, A.L. McLennan. Dad may have been right, but his theory must have been formed before we met the Hasler brothers because they were not Americans and had never been sailors, but for all the years we knew them they donated considerably to keep the UDL company afloat.

That gin was an essential ingredient in the Haslers' lives, and luckily for them, Tom was so rich that every Friday afternoon he would buy a tank of gas for Almont's car and the three brothers would drive sedately over to Cloverdale where they bought the following week's groceries, which always included at least one full case of UDL. On high days and holidays, if their liquor ration books still had coupons, they would add bottles of other types of booze as well.

I say that Almont drove sedately and I mean that too. He had an almost new Hudson car, but he never drove it over twenty miles per hour, even though the wartime speed limit was thirty. In spite of that, the car was handy for them and it was mighty handy for me too, because Tom used to hire me about twice a week to give the car a polish job, and the wages he paid were top score. On those polish days, if all three brothers agreed that it was a job well done they allowed me to target-shoot five shots from Tom's .22 pistol. That was a good deal for them because at the time a box of fifty "Whiz Bang" .22 short cartridges cost all of twenty-one cents when they could be had at all. Ammunition was not easy to come by, but Harry knew somebody who had been smart enough to load up before the war and who was now selling off some of his hoard. One of the other neighbours remarked one time that the stuff was "hot," but I never got burnt or had any other trouble with it.

Tom's pistol was a rare model, a "Stevens Game Getter" that had a twelve-inch barrel and also a detachable wire rifle stock that made it easy to shoot accurately. Within a short time I became proficient with it. After a few practice sessions I was able to outshoot all three of the Haslers. Tom also had an almost worn-out, short-barrelled .38 Smith & Wesson revolver with a cylinder so worn that sometimes it didn't rotate far enough. When it was fired that way, almost as much lead flew out the side of it as came out the barrel. For that reason we seldom used it. Besides, the accuracy was so poor that the only way a person could hit the cabin wall was if he were on the inside. It sure did make a wonderfully loud bang though, and if it was fired at night it was amazing how it flamed as much out its sides as it did out the barrel. Tom said it was getting dangerous to use. He had decided that when the present supply of ammunition was used up, he was not buying any more and would then throw the gun into the river. When he made that statement, I made a mental note to be on hand when he pitched it and I hoped it would land in a shallow part of the river.

If I wanted to work a little harder at heavier labour, like packing the water up from the creek or splitting a week's kindling, they had a real deal for me. Then I was allowed to shoot Tom's 32.20 Winchester rifle. That was a privilege because it was powerful enough to have a mild recoil and was also powerful enough to kill a deer at close range. I didn't need any persuasion to make these deals. It was mutual agreement from beginning to end, and we made them often enough that by the time I was eleven years old, people around the Elgin community were beginning to say things like, "That goddam Choate kid has become a damn good shot." On this earth there could be no reward more appreciated than to hear those words. In two more years, with my own 12-gauge shotgun, I was beginning to win hams and turkeys at the local trapshoots.

It must have been about six months after Tom and I adopted each other, we were out wandering through the fields along the Nicomekl River (it was also referred to by the locals as the "Nic") when a muskrat "plunked" in the water right beside us. Tom was still new to the area so he turned to me, who was walking guard with the 32.20, and asked, "Are there many mushrats around here?" (These Peace River men had a vocabulary that was a bit different from what I was being taught at home and school. When I asked Tom about that one time, he explained that many of the words and expressions they used were taken out of the old fur trade language called Chinook. He went on to describe how in the early white settler days there were so many different Indian languages that the fur traders made up a new jargon, a mixture of French, English, Gaelic, and every Indian language that the traders had to deal with. Tom explained all of this and then laughed as he finished it off with, "I got a hunch that everybody that uses it makes up a few words of their own and when they are repeated often enough, especially by other people, the words then become part of the language." Perhaps up in the north country that was true, but when I tried the system at school it put absolutely no A's on my schoolwork. But then, what could you expect of a schoolteacher?)

Anyway, after Tom and I watched that muskrat swim across the river, Tom planted an idea that was going to have a profound effect on the rest of my life. He turned toward the spot where the muskrat had gone and then turned to me again as he said, "If there are many of those things around here, then I would think a smart young bugger like you would be turning some of them into cash."

Cash? Now that really perked my ears up and after a few pointed questions on the subject from me, Tom decided it was rest time, so we located a comfortable-looking log to sit on. After Tom got well positioned he pulled out his gin flask, took a good long swig, wiped his mouth, capped the bottle, and then proceeded to teach the uninformed.

He started out by telling me, "Next winter when its fur is prime, the pelt on that mushrat will fetch the trapper that catches it about a dollar fifty."

I remembered now that Dad had made reference to someone else trapping muskrats, but I must have assumed that trapping was something that was only done in the north country, where the previous six months of Tom's stories were centred. It seems strange that I did not clue in sooner, but later was better than never. My slowness on the subject may have stemmed from the slant of Dad's comment, which suggested trapping was something other people did. We were farmers and that seemed to put us on a different social level. But as of that day, literally, the rat had jumped out of the bag.

"How do I go about catching them?" I asked Tom.

"Has your Dad got any number aught or number one steel traps?" Tom asked in reply.

I did not know what type of traps he was talking about, so I described the only ones I knew we had, which were wooden platform types that we set for rats and mice. Tom understood what I was referring to, but he just shook his head and advised me that even the rat trap was not big enough to do the job that needed doing.

"What other kinds of fur live around here?" Tom asked.

By this time I was catching onto the subject fast, so I rhymed off foxes, mink (though I had not seen one of these yet), squirrels, and a few bobcats that screeched in the night. Up until then I had not seen one of them either and had not really wanted to, but with the comfort of the 32.20 lying across my lap they had become a part of life that I was now ready to tackle.

For a few moments Tom seemed to be lost in thought, but he soon nodded his head towards the river again as he continued the conversation. "Ted, you are living right in the centre of a living gold mine. Why don't you take advantage of it this winter?"

It was a beautiful day to sit by the river that was becoming an outdoor classroom, and after taking another good pull on the flask, Tom began giving me my first lesson on how to become rich, just like he had done. In this school the pupil willingly moved up closer.

"All you need to get started here is about a half dozen traps," Tom began. "That would be three number aughts for squirrels and three number ones for these mushrats and mink. And sometimes when you are lucky, a number one will hold a fox too. Don't bother with the bobcats because they require a bigger trap. Besides, they are hard to skin and they ain't worth much after you do."

"But Tom, I don't know anything about how to do all this. Will you show me how to get started?" I asked him.

"Oh sure I will," Tom replied, "as long as you do as I tell you. And you can keep all the money that's made from the pelts too. But you gotta remember, it's you that's going to do all of the work."

This was turning out to be the greatest lesson I had ever listened to, but I still had a few more questions for Tom. "How much is a mink or fox worth?" I asked him.

"Oh, a good mink, the last time I sold some, got me as high as twenty-five dollars and a red fox is worth about ten dollars," he informed me.

I remembered another animal that I had heard there were a few of in the area, so I asked Tom about them. "How about coons, Tom. Are they worth anything?"

Tom thought for a moment and then replied, "I dunno. There are none up north and the only one I ever seen was in a circus." He sat there and had a good belly laugh as he took another long pull on the bottle. I got the impression that coons probably weren't worth much, so I laughed them off too. But Tom still had more information to share. "If you are lucky enough to catch a cross or silver fox, they can sometimes fetch as much as $200. Too bad there ain't any marten around here because they are real easy to catch and are always worth over a hundred dollars. God, a marten is easier to catch than a bushtailed packrat," he reminisced.

Do you think this kid was hooked? I was becoming so excited that I could hardly breathe, so I asked Tom, "How much do traps cost, Tom?"

"Oh, somewhere between fifty cents and a dollar," he answered.

That was an answer to ponder. Perhaps that was not much money for someone as rich as Tom, but for me it was a different matter. With bated breath I whispered another question to him. "Tom, did you bring any traps down from the north country with you?"

Just as I feared, he apologetically shook his head and admitted, "I left every one of them up there. It seems strange that we never even brought a few of the small ones along for catching those goddam wharf rats up at The Shack, but it's one of those things we never thought about as we packed up to move down south here." For a moment he sat there quietly shaking his head at his absent-mindedness. I can still remember wondering how anybody as smart as Tom Hasler could be so short-sighted and forgetful. At least he wasn't totally forgetful, because he did remember to bring most of his guns and I was sure thankful for that.

For the rest of the day as we roamed the fields and bush, Tom pointed out all of the most likely looking places for me to set my traps. We even stopped a few times as he used his big Hudson's Bay hunting knife to carve out "cubby holes" in the stream banks where I would later place pieces of fish for bait and set a camouflaged trap. These sets would be for the mink and, if I was lucky, silver foxes. The muskrats and squirrels would be easier to catch, Tom said, as the rats were living in the dike and had obvious holes and runs. Tom said I wouldn't even need to cover the traps. The squirrels had their dens and runs in hollow trees and logs, and he said they would be the easiest to handle of all. "I'll teach you to skin a rat or squirrel in less than three minutes," Tom promised.

As we wandered through the bush, my mind was in a total quandary and it was all about money. Here I was on the brink of becoming immensely rich, but the seed money I needed to begin hauling in the wealth was in terribly short supply. I did still have a piggy bank at home that held my entire financial resources, and that was the problem. At the last count that I could remember there had been something just short of five dollars, but since then there had been a few five-cent extractions for buying pop and ice-cream cones, so I was now in a fearful sweat over what a newer count might reveal. But somehow and some way, something had to be done as the difference between the gains from picking spuds and from trapping were so far apart that I knew my spud-picking days were over. At least I hoped they were.

When I returned home that evening the financial problem had still not been solved, so at dinner I hesitantly broached the subject to my parents. From earlier conversations with Dad on the subject of job preferences, I was not all that surprised by his reaction to my proposed new venture. He was completely thumbs down on it. He was a strict believer in what he considered to be “honest” labour and he did not consider trapping to be in that category, though I do not remember his rationale for that position. As I was no brighter in those days than I am now, I did not help my cause by pointing out to him the probable difference between what could be made trapping and what could be made picking somebody else’s spuds. And this huge difference could be realized by a small investment in a mere six steel traps. Are you familiar with the meaning of the phrase “a father’s cold stare”?

This subject divided our family. One of my older sisters was still living at home and as she and I were quite competitive, she immediately jumped in on Dad’s side of the argument. What really surprised me, though, was that Mom turned out to be enthusiastic about the idea. It’s possible that this was because she had been raised in the Cypress Hills of Saskatchewan and she could still remember when she and her two sisters made their spending money by relieving gophers of their tails for a penny apiece. Now that I had Mom as a lukewarm ally, I smartened up in a hurry and began using that little lever for all it was worth.

Her support should not have been so much of a surprise, because she and I had many other agreements over values. One of the major ones was that Mom was much more favourably inclined towards my best friend Tom Hasler than Dad was. Dad often referred to Tom as an “old ginny,” and the way he said it did not sit well with me because I knew that the implication was somehow wrong. One time when Dad was talking that way over dinner—another one of those veggie affairs—I piped right up in defence of the Hasler crew by countering, “So what if they drink gin? At least they are richer than we are and they have meat with every meal too.”

I can still remember that conversation as clearly as if it happened last week, especially Dad’s reaction to it. He sat there staring at me for a moment or so as his face went greyer, then he turned his eyes towards the window and silently stared at something out there for a long while. At the same time, Mom must have remembered something that needed doing out in the kitchen, so Dad and I were left there at the table alone together. Do you believe in "deafening silence"? There really is such a thing, and my ears still tend to burn and ring every time the memory drifts by. That silent lecture was the worst one I ever received. It's for sure that nobody had to order me to clean up my boiled onions that night. I even volunteered to help my sister Pat with the dishes—an unheard-of offer that she of course refused to accept. God, that room became so stifling that I was almost afraid to keep breathing for fear someone would notice me sitting there. Just what is a kid supposed to do under circumstances like those?

After that I discovered the best way to handle the trapping subject was to avoid even mentioning it. Don't get the idea that the plan was dying on the vine because it was anything but. It was still being debated at The Shack on a daily basis, and over there, there was no such thing as a dissenting opinion. At The Shack, everything was green-lighted and it was all being left up to me as to how and when I could throw the switch.

There is no question that was the time when my life's decision was made. Even though I was only eight years old, my mind had clicked to the fact that hunting and trapping were going to be my future. Just as soon as I could legally quit school—which would be another agonizing eight-year lifetime away—it was going to be good-bye to family and friends as I headed for the real fur and game country, taking over the trails and places that Tom and Harry had to leave because they had lived too long and could not cut the mustard of that life anymore. Everybody at The Shack was in agreement that all this should be so, and from then on the boys spent our time together getting me primed up for the golden days to come. By the time I reached the magical age of sixteen, Tom and Harry would have taught me all they knew and I would be well prepared to blaze my own trails. They assured me over and over that there was still a lifetime of country up there among the rivers and bush that no whiteman had yet seen.

Oh, the stories and teachings those old trailmen had for me! The Hasler boys were forever talking about places that had the most interesting sounding names—Omineca, Fort George, Peace River, Fort Nelson, Athabasca, Yukon, Pouce Coupe (which they pronounced "Poos Coopy"), Fort Simpson, and an endless number of other places that Tom showed me on some of his maps. It sounded like there were forts all over the north country and I could hardly wait to get there. The Hudson's Bay Fur Company was always in their conversation too. We were beginning to learn about it in school, which confirmed the fact that these men spoke the truth. And right there on some of those maps that Tom had there were large blank spots, sometimes with light notations describing them as "unsurveyed" and sometimes, for the headwaters of rivers and large creeks, as "unknown." How much more evidence was needed? There was a whole world up there just waiting for me, and sometimes I would wake up at night, worried that some other kid might get there ahead of me.

There were hundreds of stories that came with these place names and since all three of the brothers were retired, there was always somebody at The Shack who could regale me for hours on end with sworn true experiences. There were countless trapline stories, stories of having to hunt moose for the winter meat supply, and stories of having to kill any number of caribou before winter set in so they could feed their dogs (my poor dog had to live mostly on boiled potatoes, as did Oink, our pet pig). As they told these stories they talked as though it was a lot of hard work, which must have been one of their little jokes that I could never understand. Then there were stories of how the wolves would follow the dog-teams, sometimes for days at a time, and a person had to sleep all night half awake, with a loaded Winchester inside the blanket roll to keep it warm so it never misfired when it was needed in a hurry. And there were people stories of barroom fights, lots of goddam good women, solved murders, and unsolved murders from throughout that wonderful country up there. Some of those murderers beat the rap, but the neighbours knew the truth. A man had to be damn careful what he said and did around those murderers because there was always a danger that they might try it again. The boys advised me that a short-barrelled pistol was handy to have at times like that.

One of the stories I made them tell many times was about a trapper in the Athabasca country who resolved one of those neighbour problems when a killer who had beat a rap down south moved up north to become something much worse—a "trapline jumper." What the "good guy" trapper did after he tired of the other fellow's shenanigans was go to the jumper's cabin, supposedly for a friendly visit, and as soon as the goddam thief turned his back, his neighbour just swatted him across the side of his head with the back of an axe and then fed the body to the dogs. Tom and Harry assured me that everybody else who lived in the area was relieved it was done, and not even the police asked too many questions. Tom was really good at telling this story. When he got to the part about swatting the thief with the axe, he would stand right in front of me as he demonstrated exactly how the trapper swung the axe and then he would scratch the side of my head to show exactly where the axe hit. That story was enough to make a person's scalp tingle, and sometimes my body got itchy all over. One time after Tom retold the story, Harry, who was sitting in his chair comfortably ginned and nodding in agreement, reminded everybody, "Yeah, and for all the rest of his life that guy never again had to make or buy a single drop of booze."

One subject that I never picked up on too well came up one afternoon when the stories were about long, cold winters, being snowed in for days at a time, and camping out on cold, lonely trails. A person could get real shivery listening to those experiences. During a lull in the conversation Tom said to me, "When you get up in that country, one of the smartest things you can do is make up with an Indian girl and take her along for company."

I could not understand the reasoning for this and said so, as my entire northward plans had always been to go and do it all alone. When I challenged Tom's suggestion, the others teamed up with him. Almont, with a big grin on his face, informed me, "By the time you are sixteen you will understand what Tom is referring too." They all began chuckling away like a bunch of old hens until Harry added his two bits' worth by saying, "Yup, there is nobody else that can tan moose and caribou hides better than an Indian girl." At that remark they all sat in their chairs and rocked around, suffering from convulsive belly laughs that had to be cured by what looked like about a double-sized pull apiece, straight from the bottle.

Let me tell you, though, when those stories started flowing it became mighty hard for a kid to break away for home or be bothered going to school next day. Obviously prosperity and social acceptance were up there in the north, waiting to be taken advantage of. I often wondered what it took to make the aging clock tick faster.

Those stories did have one positive consequence at school, because they did bring out in me an intense interest in maps and geography. They even gave me a good grounding in what was called “Social Studies,” which I remember covered a pretty broad spectrum. Those northern stories gave me enough background knowledge to contradict and argue with several of the teachers until their backs were against the wall. The stories were no help with subjects like math and science, as the teachers that taught those subjects were of the opinion that hunting and trapping were not worthwhile occupations. This was still a time when almost all teachers were encouraging pupils to take up professions and trades and become doctors, lawyers, engineers, nurses, and teachers. The ultimate goal, they told us, was to get into “white collar” jobs.

Well, that was their opinion, but it’s for sure that they were not able to persuade everybody to follow their lead. I already knew as much about the locations of many of Canada’s northern towns and rivers as the teachers did, and sometimes more, and they did not seem to appreciate being challenged by me. Some of them got back at me with their dry maths and European history, but I already knew I was not destined to need much of that information. When it came to deciding what subjects to try and do well in, how many kids in North America were going to benefit from knowing the sequences of all those long-dead European kings? Almost everybody I met who had been to Europe told me that the only way to go over there was with a rifle on my shoulder. But try telling things like that to a teacher. Sometimes I would have been better off if I just kept my mouth shut, but that was something I seldom did. For the life of me I cannot remember how I made out with English, but somehow I did learn to read. Writing I’m not so sure about.

Getting back to the trap problem, it was sometime after the cooling-off period that followed the ordeal with Dad at the dinner table that I was invited to accompany him into Vancouver for the day, probably a Saturday. At the time he was still using one of his Model A Fords, and when we went to the city he always parked on Cordova Street. I do not remember why Dad was going into Vancouver that day, but it may have been to attend some of the International Woodworkers of America union meetings that he was involved in. He also attended meetings in New Westminster, where his union hall was located. Many times I had to accompany him whether I wanted to or not because if Mom or Pat were not at home, we could not afford a kid sitter. I was made to come into the hall, which had the hardest wooden benches that have ever been made, and was always instructed to "Sit right there and keep your mouth shut." That is not the easiest thing for an eight-year-old kid to do, especially when all the adults there ever did was argue and talk, argue and talk and argue and talk. And all about nothing interesting.

When we went into Vancouver, things were much different and Dad would give me the freedom of the street as long as I never got out of sight of the car. As a matter of fact, I was supposed to "keep an eye" on it. I think there were a couple of reasons he gave me this freedom. For one thing, Vancouver streets then were still safe for kids. For another, he knew I was not going to get out of sight of one of the most interesting and important buildings in that city—a large corner store that bore the name of "Harkley and Haywood Sporting Goods." At that time it was the largest such store in British Columbia and the owners boasted that they kept the largest collection of both new and used guns on the West Coast. There was another smaller and similar emporium kitty-corner from it. The name of that store was "Sissons." It was more into fishing tackle than guns, but it too was well worth browsing through. As far as this kid was concerned, there were always enough interesting things in those two stores to occupy a mind. The unionists could sit on their hard benches until the cows came home, but whatever time that took, when they were finished they would find the "eye" was still right there within sight of that car. Considering the amount of time I spent at the counters and windows of those two stores, I'll bet the salesmen often wished as much as I did that I was ten years older and had pockets full of money. Just the same, though, they were always mighty good to me and between the moneyed customers that they did have, they spent a lot of time seeding what they must have sensed was going to be future growth.

This particular Saturday was going to be different for all of us, as I had not arrived to buy fifteen cents' worth of fish hooks. Instead I had my entire worldly fortune, which amounted to around four dollars, all of it in change. It did not seem to matter how many times I counted it, the total always came close to that same four dollars, give or take a few cents. With that much money in my pocket I was able to boldly, brazenly, and truthfully walk right past the hook and fly counter and go straight to the back of the store where there was a small sign that said "Trapping Supplies." It turned out to be lucky timing for me. That day the store was short on cash customers, so I was able to have the exclusive use of a salesman for about two hours, which allowed me to feel and weigh every trap in the place. By then the decisions had been made and my purchase turned out to be four number aught Victor traps that cost thirty-five cents each and two number ones that cost sixty cents each. There was no sales tax either.

Up to that day I had never handled traps like these, but the salesman took the time to show me how to set a number aught and then reach up from underneath the trap with a finger, pull down on the trigger pan, and set the trap off without getting caught. It appears that I was a slow learner back then too. The first time I tried doing it, something went wrong and the trap caught its first victim. A loud yelp from me brought every other clerk and customer in the store, and they all began chipping in to further my education. God, I had never had so much appreciated attention in my life. When I explained to the audience what I intended to do with these traps, every person there was in total agreement. It all reconfirmed everything the crew at The Shack had been telling me. When I explained to my new friends just who and what Tom Hasler was, one of those men informed me, "You are a goddam lucky kid to have a friend like that guy Tom." Nobody had to tell me that, but it was nice to hear just the same. When I walked out the door of Harkley and Haywood with all that moral support behind me, I burned a lot of mental bridges.

That last statement is not an idle description of my situation because with those traps in a brown paper bag under my arm, there was no getting around the fact that I was soon going to have to deal with the next obstacle, my parents, head on. Even though Dad had willingly let me come into the city with him, I had neglected to tell him or Mom why I wanted to come. Now that the initial deed was done, I was in a great sweat trying to think of a way to gently broach the subject to Dad, who I knew was going to be the major stumbling block.

As it turned out, I got to the car before he did so rather than hide the traps in the rumble seat and not mention them, I decided to get it over with at once and laid them all out on the front seat where they could be felt and admired. While sitting there waiting for Dad's return, I could not resist the temptation to go through all of the trap-setting rituals again and after clipping my fingers in the aughts a few more times, I thought I was proficient enough to try the number ones, which were much stronger in the spring. After building up enough nerve, I began struggling with the spring by bracing it between my knees. This was not quite working and I must have been totally engrossed in the problem because I was suddenly jolted back into the world when I realized that Dad was standing right there with the car door open, watching me. When our eyes met he asked, "Where did you get those things?"

"I bought them at Harkley and Haywood with my own money," I replied.

There was a not particularly pleasant expression on his face as he inquired, "And how much did they cost?"

He was my Dad, so I told him the truth.

"And how much money do you have left now?" he queried further.

"Over a dollar and forty cents," I stated defensively.

"So you have spent almost all of your spud money on that pile of scrap, have you?" he stated.

"Tom says that the first mink I catch will be worth more than twenty-five dollars," was my reply to that.

Dad still just stood there staring at me and the traps until he coarsely whispered, "That old son-of-a-bitch." My Dad hardly ever swore and I did not like to hear him do it, especially when it was directed towards my very best friend.

For a few more moments Dad stood shaking his head, dividing his stare between me and the Harkley and Haywood store. It suddenly dawned on me that he might actually be thinking of sending me back over there with the traps to beg for the return of my money. My heart almost came to a standstill as I prayed that if there really was a God in Heaven, surely he would not allow my own father to force me to go through such a humiliating ordeal. Before my breathing stopped altogether or the sky fell, Dad broke the impasse by shaking his head in defeat as he reached under the seat for the crank. As he straightened up he said to me, "Okay, it's your money, but there is an old saying about things like this and it goes 'A fool and his money are soon parted.' Some fools spend it on booze and others spend it on useless junk." He then cranked up the engine and we were off for home and he never mentioned the subject directly again.

So it turned out it wasn't such a hard deal after all, and when we arrived home with Dad half neutralized, Mom was no problem at all. Even though I was still not in the same league as the northern trappers, I sensed that I had been launched into a wonderful new destiny. It's surprising how a person gets a gut feeling that way and from then on somehow takes the right fork on every trail because he knows he's onto the real thing.

After we got home, it took me all of three minutes to grab my new tools and sail over to The Shack so Tom and Harry could look them over and nod their approval. Tom said these were the best-looking traps he had ever seen, as they had some improvements built into them that his older ones never had. Talk about lucky decisions. Over the next few days the boys taught me how to boil the machine oil off the traps in a bucket of water that was half full of cedar needles. After that we buried them in a hole and covered them with cow dung, where they would be left until they were "cured." As Tom had to tell me several times, we still had to wait a few months for the fur on the animals to "prime up," as late September was way too early in these southern climes to catch the best fur.

For some reason, important things hardly ever proceed as easily as they should and in this case there turned out to be a couple more hurdles to cross before we could get started. The first one was that both the Haslers and Dad said there was actually such a thing as an "opening day" to the trapping season, just like there was for fishing, hunting, and going to school. The other thing was that trapping required a licence. There were licences for hunting and fishing too, but as I had never had to buy a licence to hunt or fish, it did not make any sense that I should now have to buy one to trap. Somebody mentioned that a trapping license cost ten dollars, which would have sent all of our plans into a tailspin. To avoid that problem, everybody but Dad agreed that I could probably catch as much fur without a licence as I could with one. That made good profitable sense and it did become the final decision.

Dad still would not let up. The next stumbling block he set was to inform me that there was already an adult trapper using the area we intended to set up shop in. Furthermore, this guy had been established there for a few years and he actually had a licence to be there, something Dad emphasized that I still did not have and that I had better start thinking about it. Most of this stuff was falling on unreceptive ears, but after continuous mealtime bombardments I realized it was something that had to be resolved somehow, and if it could not be done in our house there was always the one next door, so that's where I took the problem.

I decided to broach this subject to the crew on a Friday afternoon when all three brothers had just returned from Cloverdale with the following week's supply of groceries and gin. Friday was steak night at The Shack and as always, I was hopeful about being invited for supper. This time it looked like a good bet. I had volunteered to help pack the grub into The Shack and had been snoopy enough to note that they had remembered to buy four full-sized steaks, which right then began a new surge of volunteering from me. By the time I had filled the wood box and topped up all the water buckets with trips down to the creek, nobody had started to cook supper but the UDL was flowing freely. They already had about three quarters of the first bottle under their belts, so everything was shaping up towards a good night of storytelling.

Old Tom's Shack was not big, perhaps twelve feet wide by twenty feet long. The wood cookstove, table, and four chairs were at one end and there were three cots set up lengthwise at the other end, though these were never referred to as cots because they were really bunks. With the exception of Almont, these old sourdoughs had never slept in a bed in their lives as even during the best of times, the cabins they slept in had no more than bunks if the men were lucky. Lots of times they just rolled out on the floor. Up north they never used sheets. Everybody simply packed their own bedroll everywhere they went, either a Hudson's Bay blanket or an Indian rabbitskin robe. In more recent times, people were taking to these newfangled things called sleeping bags, which everybody agreed were a pretty damn good invention. When the Haslers had been out on the trails and rivers, they simply rolled up in one of those blankets under a canoe or riverboat in summer. In the winters when they had to "siwash it," they used a tarp strung between two trees to reflect heat from their campfires. When it got really cold, like down around sixty or seventy below zero, they might add the luxury of a tanned moosehide over top of their rabbitskin robes. They knew how to make those situations sound like the most exciting kind of fun too. But now that they had moved down into these southern latitudes, they always slept in these bunks and even though they did still have their rabbitskin and moosehide bedrolls, I noticed that all three of them seemed to prefer their Hudson's Bay Four Pointers. As Almont said on several occasions, it seemed like age might be softening them up a bit, and even Tom admitted that it might be so.

Just the same, the way the boys told those stories made it awfully hard for a kid to ever want to sleep in a bed again. One time when they had sparked my enthusiasm up to its top limits, I decided to give the cabin-floor system a try in my own bedroom. It did not seem to have exactly the same comfort they described as it took a lot of rolling and flopping around before I was able to go to sleep. Perhaps the fir floorboards in our house were harder than the ones made of spruce and pine up north. When I asked Tom and Harry about that the next day, they told me that it just takes a bit of getting used to, and anyway, a person should not get into the habit of sleeping too soundly lest a bear or wolverine tries raiding the camp or cabin. Tom further suggested that if I wanted to indulge in the most comfortable sleep in the bush, I should locate a bushy tree that had a deep pile of squirrel shavings under it, scratch out a level trough in them, and then lay my bedroll down into it.

"Yup, there ain't nothing quite like bedding down with a bunch of squirrels," Harry agreed. They made it sound so cozy that I could hardly wait to try it.

Almont hardly ever slept at The Shack as he had a wife and home over at Newton, about ten miles away, and he would make every effort to get back there before dark. At the speed he drove, that could take a while, and there were a few times when he got a little too deep into the UDL and spent the night with Tom. When that happened, his wife would somehow ground him when he finally got back home and we wouldn't see him all week until Friday afternoon, when it was necessary to take his brothers over to Cloverdale for a load of grub and other necessities. He had a couple of driving experiences that spooked him up a bit. One time on his way home he drove into a flooded ditch and later told us that he damn near drowned. The accident scratched up his car a bit too, and that seemed to upset him more than coming close to drowning. A farmer with a big tractor had to come and pull him out and help get the car restarted. Another time he must have become confused in the fog or something because he ended up sleeping in the car. When he woke up next morning, he discovered he was parked in front of the liquor store at Cloverdale and there were a bunch of kids staring in the window at him. Later on, when he was telling us about that experience, he said that perhaps he should lay off the UDL for a while. Harry's laughing reply was, "I'll just bet you will."

That wife of his was something else. She never did fit into our crew and I do not believe she even tried to. I could never figure out why this was, because anytime she came to visit, all of us were on our very best behaviour. Tom and Harry would even stop swearing. On my level, I never did refer to her by name. She was always "Mrs. Hasler." I sure never had to refer to the brothers as "Mister" Hasler, so as you can see, we on our side did our best to keep the welcome mat out front and cleaned up a bit, but she never reciprocated. At least not the way you would think she should have.

Luckily she never came over too often, as when she did she could be a nuisance. She seemed to cast some sort of spell over all of the Hasler men. When she visited, the very first thing she would do was go snooping into everything in The Shack, even though nobody invited her to do so. She would stoop so low as to go rummaging around under the bunks where the boys kept their private things cached. When she had finished doing that, she would still not be satisfied but would grab a broom, chase all us men outside with it, and proceed to "shovel the place out," as she put it. She would even move the bunks around and stir up and sweep up everything she found under them that did not suit her values, which were obviously not the same as ours.

Some of Tom and Harry's comments from before and after those visits made me wonder if anybody had ever actually invited her to come, especially since she had one flaw that was so bad the rest of us had to remain on continuous guard against it. Mrs. Hasler was a teetotaler. So was I, but there was a difference. In her case, she was evangelistic with her theories about the evils of alcohol and she could and often did defend them vehemently. She didn't just defend them. She preferred to attack with them! For instance, every time she came to The Shack she would almost instantly begin to lecture the crew about the evils of our ways, especially the one she could smell. Nobody ever tried conning her into believing that the stuff had not been there. That UDL gin was so strong, and enough of it had been spilt on the floor and bunks, that in self-defence I kept the door open as much as possible. What the place must have smelled like to someone like her is hard to imagine. One time when she was there and had made the mistake of closing the door for too long, she finally threw it open again herself as she exclaimed, "How can you people stand this place? It just REEKS of that poison." She hit that problem pretty close to the mark. A few times when she went into one of those anti-booze frenzies she actually tore around the building breaking some of the bottles. I can remember wondering why Tom and Harry let her get away with it. They often acted like they were afraid of her. But not all of us were.

By contrast, my opinion was that alcohol appeared to be an excellent social mellower as in our crew there was never an argument about anything. We all agreed with everybody else and once in a while, when we could not quite swallow another person's opinion or advice, we laughed at them. That made more sense than to fight about it the way some of the other old people I knew did.

My permanent throne at The Shack was the chair right beside the door. That was where the guns were stored, but there was more than that one reason I sat there. Part of my job was to keep a sharp lookout for Almont's car's approach. When I did spot it I would quickly climb up a few rungs on the ladder that was propped against the roof in case of chimney fires, high enough so I could see into the car when it turned off the highway. I was to watch out for Mrs. Hasler. If she was in the car I would sing out, "HERE SHE COMES!" At that signal we all rushed around the cabin, caching the UDL and whatever other contraband was within sight. She had no objection to guns, so was not totally unreasonable.

I got pretty good at this lookout job, but one afternoon I slipped up. Tom and Harry were comfortably inebriated and half asleep in their chairs and were not capable of moving too fast, and I was engrossed in cleaning the Winchester when all of a sudden Almont's car, with her in it, pulled up right beside The Shack. It may have been a weekend because underneath my chair beside the door was the UDL box with almost a full week's supply in it. Somebody had to make decisions and do something real fast, so this time I did it all. I tipped my chair over, dropped the rifle, grabbed the box that still had eight or nine bottles in it, and headed out the door and away from the car. Mrs. Hasler was not very spry, so by the time I cleared the step she was just getting the car door open. She was still close enough to see what I had in my arms. I only slowed enough to give Almont the benefit of a fast nod of greeting and never bothered looking at his wife as I headed out over the creek bank into the bush below. Just as I was clearing the edge of that bank, Mrs. Hasler began screaming something at me that sounded like, "Teddy, you get right back here with that!" By then I was enough jumps ahead of her that it affected my hearing, so I just kept going down over the edge where it was impossible to hear anything from up top. After caching the evidence deep in a clump of devil's club, it seemed like a good idea to take my leave and go home to work on my chores for a while rather than go back to The Shack and listen to sermons that nobody wanted to hear anyway.

For the rest of the afternoon, every hour or so I'd sneak back up the trail aways to where I could check whether the car was still parked there. Toward the end of the afternoon it did leave, so I ventured back to The Shack. When I pushed the door open I watched Tom and Harry move faster than I ever thought them capable of. They both literally bounded to the door as Harry exclaimed, "Where is it? Did you break any of the bottles?"

They were well sobered up by then, so after I assured them that everything was safe and sound we all went down to the creek to retrieve the groceries. It took the boys three good swigs apiece on the way back to The Shack to return to normal, and by then they were so appreciative of how things had turned out that as soon as Harry plopped down into his regular roost he said to Tom, "By God Tom, for that piece of work you give Ted a full twenty rounds with the Winchester."

"I sure as hell will," Tom replied. "If she had of made it to the door any faster, we would have had the driest week since we left home. You know Harry, a call as close as that one was makes me think that as soon as Almont is allowed out of his house again, we had better get an extra case and keep it down there by the creek."

Harry nodded in agreement as he replied, "Yup." The following week they actually did get a second case, too.

There were other times when Mrs. Hasler arrived during the week when I wasn't around to give the warning signal. Then she caught the crew red-handed and she really used to lay it onto them. I arrived at The Shack a couple of times when she was in full rage. Once she was so fired up about something that she actually grabbed the broom and began dusting Tom over his head and shoulders with it, which resulted in all of us men making a run for the door. At the time I had been filling the kindling box, but that turned out to be no protection from the likes of her because she took a swing at me too, screaming that she knew I was growing up to become as bad as the rest because she had just discovered a bottle of whisky cached in the kindling box and I had not had the decency to tell her about it. She then made a great show of marching outside with that bottle, set it on the chopping block, then took a great roundhouse swing at it with the hatchet that resulted in all of us men getting showered with glass and whisky. Rationed booze too! And do you know what those rough tough old trappers did then? Not one of them said a word! As soon as Mrs. Hasler went back into The Shack, one of the men took a small cardboard box and began picking up the shards of glass and dropping them into it. Pretty soon all four of us were doing it, though we didn't look at each other or say a word. Strange.

I never did get to like Mrs. Hasler much. I learned to tolerate her presence when it was necessary, mostly out of respect for her relationship to the rest. But The Shack could have done just as well or better without her, because to my way of thinking she was not very bright. That was driven deeper home one day when she had arrived to go through her regular procedure of "shovelling out The Shack." All of us men had been moved outside and had taken our chairs with us. Mine was tipped back against the building, right beside the door, and the other three had set up in a semicircle facing me and the door. This was a dry party, but the crew were gleefully enlightening me about some of their past experiences when Mrs. Hasler stuck her nose out the door and said to them, referring to me, "What are you fellows putting this poor tyke up to now?"

TYKE? I was sitting there minding my own business, practising speed loading Tom's .38, and she comes up with a question like that? Does any sane person make a statement like that within earshot of a ten-year-old trapper who has a loaded pistol in his hand? That woman gambled with destiny. I can still remember the situation was so tense for me that I began getting the trembling shakes, but luckily I was able to control myself enough to give her the benefit of the doubt, which was to pretend that I did not understand the implication. Mrs. Hasler had never been high on my preference list, but after that day she practically ceased to exist.

Getting back to the dilemma of the other trapper and the trapping licence, though, that Friday afternoon was shaping up to be a good time to resolve it. There came a break between stories and the boys had to "swig up" before getting into another, so I broached the subject to them then. When I mentioned it, they stopped talking and laughing and just sat there with their tin cups of gin in their hands (they never used anything as frivolous as glasses). They had strange looks of curiosity on their faces that did not seem to bode well, and I could feel my heart beginning to slide downwards, landing down around my gumboots somewhere.

Just the looks on those faces told me that there was going to be a rough road ahead.

Harry was the first to respond. He stared right at me and said, "The hell you say."

Tom took a bit longer and his answer was, "Well, I'll be a son-of-a-bitch."

This was getting worse by the second and the possibility of a bad outcome was making my mouth go dry. Tom was thoughtfully shaking his head as he asked for confirmation. "So your Dad says there is a licensed trapper working this area, eh?"

"Yup," I answered, just like I knew it couldn't possibly make any difference.

Then Harry cut back in by saying, "The dumb son-of-a-bitch. Who the hell would pay ten bucks for a licence to trap in a place like this?"

Tom was still sitting there shaking his head as he answered back, "Yeah, but the bastard might turn out to be a problem."

Oh, oh. This conversation seemed to be going into all of the wrong directions and it spun my mind into overdrive. The only thing that surfaced was the story of the unwanted trapper problem in the Athabasca country. That brought up more questions, as I did not know if the same solution would work at Elgin. For one thing, this other trapper was an adult and much bigger than me and up to that time I had never swatted anybody with the back of an axe. I can still remember mentally sweating as I wondered what would happen if I didn't hit him hard enough or worse yet, if I missed him altogether? The three of us sat in silence for a few moments. Then Almont returned from a long contemplation in the outhouse and went straight to his customary chair and plopped down. Before anyone else could butt in with more negative comments, I asked for his opinion too, hoping he could brighten things up a bit. I shouldn't have asked.

Almont didn't answer right away as he was busy with the priority of a quick catch-up, taking a long gurgling pull straight from the bottle and then filling his mug. He then nodded towards me as he also confirmed, "Yeah, you might have a problem all right."

Harry cut back in again as he asked of nobody in particular, "Do you guys think they would jail an eight-year-old kid for poaching?"

"What the hell do you mean, go to jail?" Tom countered. "Why just look at that kid. His legs is long enough that he can outrun any Game Warden in the country."

"As long as he stays off the roads he isn't going to meet any Game Wardens," Almont informed us.

"So there you are," Tom stated. "All Ted has to do is stay away from the rats in the ditches along the highway and out of sight from any of the other roads."

"Yup," Harry said. "All he has to learn to do is not let the Game Warden lay a hand on him or see his face, so his legs is the answer. And anyway, I've never seen a Game Warden who could shoot straight enough to slow anybody down."

At that remark Tom began chuckling as he reminded us, "Seen one, why hell Harry, you ain't even heard of one."

Poaching! Running! Shooting! Slowing down! I began sitting up a little straighter in my chair because these were subjects that had never been discussed this way before. It's hard to remember if "becoming scared" was the right description of my feelings just then, but "becoming breathlessly interested" certainly was, because these guys were talking about ME!

"Well, that takes care of the Game Warden," Harry admitted, "but what happens when he meets the other trapper on a narrow dike?"

Before any of the others could answer, I piped up with the suggestion I had figured out. "If I meet him and there ain't no room to run, I'll just drill him with the long-barrelled pistol and then roll him into the river." I knew that had to be the best solution because it was almost as good as the axe and dog deal that had been used up in the north country.

It did not seem to be appreciated by my friends, however, as they all stopped talking and sat there giving me strange-looking stares. As Almont drained his mug and began unscrewing the top from a new bottle to refill it, he casually said to Tom, "You know Tom, the old lady mentioned to me once that if this kid was to ever get into any trouble from hanging around here, you might get charged as an accomplice."

"What the hell is an accomplice?" laughed Tom.

Almont then went into a long windy explanation of a lot of stupid, dumb-sounding things that I couldn't understand and nobody wanted to listen to anyway, but just to be polite we did. There was a long silence from the other two, and the way Tom was staring at me with that squinty-eyed look he used when he was in deep thought warned me that something ominous could come out of Almont's information. The silence was so bad that not one of them thought to imbibe in a single swig when Almont wound down.

Tom finally broke the impasse. He nodded to me as he said, "Teddy, from now on I don't want you taking any of the guns out into the bush unless one of us is with you. And for sure, don't you shoot at ANYTHING unless we say it's okay."

Oh, no. How could anybody's luck turn so sour so fast? My gumboots were hardly big enough to hold everything that dropped. It felt like my heart, liver, and brains had all gone down. And it all had to do with some stupid thing *that woman* had said. Why she had to be as bad as or worse than any teacher that ever lived. What could be lower and how low is low? And come to think about it, every teacher I ever had to deal with was a woman too. It began me wondering if there could be any significance to this. The thoughts made for confusion though, because my mother was also a woman, but for some reason she was different.

The long silence in The Shack was beginning to make me feel squirmy until Tom emerged from deep thought and swept most of our problems out the door. "I know what we'll do," he told us. "Ted will just start trapping like we already planned and if the Game Warden or the other trapper is able to catch him, then we'll just have Almont drive us into Vancouver to visit one of them sharp lawyers that's always getting those city slicker murderers off the hook. And by God, I'll pay for it too," Tom emphasized. "There are a couple of those shysters in there that are so good they claim to have never lost a client to the gallows. One of them goes under the name of Angel Branca and the other one is more honest and goes under the handle of John Bull KC. I dunno what the KC stands for, but it's probably to do with being Kind to Crooks or some such thing. And by God, I got the case already figured out too," Tom continued as he leaned towards the rest of us who were right out on the edges of our chairs. At least I know that I was.

Nobody said a word while Tom drew a good pull from the UDL. Then he proceeded to enlighten us with the verdict. "Ted is going to trap the mushrats out of the dike and creek on my property. As we all know, that other trapper ain't doing a very good job of it cause there are still rat holes all over the place down there. So from now on I'm taking Ted in as my working partner and his job is to catch enough of those rats so they don't wreck my dike and let it wash out because, by God, I'm a farmer now and I got a right to protect my property from those goddam mushrats. Why hell, I even have to pay special taxes for that dike and they ain't cheap either, so I know damn well that there ain't no judge or jury that's going to jail my partner for protecting what I'm being taxed for. Why, some of those foxes down there have dug bigger holes than the rats have, so the same goes for them too. And if he happens to catch one of those twenty-five-dollar mink, then we'll just tell the city slicker judge that they're dike diggers too."

The other two brothers sat there staring at Tom for a few moments until Harry nodded in agreement and said, "Well if you really want to do it, I guess it would work out about like that."

Almont finally came back on board too as he nodded in approval and added, "With a lawyer, you can get away with anything."

So it was settled. And with everybody in agreement again, Tom handed the half-full bottle of UDL to Harry, who took a swig and refilled his mug before handing it to Almont, who did the same. When it got back to Tom there was only one swig left, which he downed with a justly flourish. Now that the problem was settled back into all the right channels again, it wasn't long before the boys were laughing and remembering stories that they hadn't remembered for years.

Just the same, for me that was a mighty close call and what I remember now is the wonderful glowing feeling that overcame me that afternoon as I resettled onto my throne and realized for a final certainty that my partner Tom Hasler was the smartest man on this earth. There could be no other way for it. Why he was smarter than any teacher ever heard of because when you start to think about it, how many of them could have resolved a situation like that as fast and easily as he did? Why I'll bet that Tom Hasler was smarter than Roy Rogers and Jesus Christ combined.

Sometime later in the fall, Tom finally said it was "time," which meant I should go and dig the traps out of the manure pile. Then we headed down to the Nicomekl together. He showed me exactly where and how to lay the traps in the burrows where the muskrats travelled, and we set two of them up on tree branches, baited with apple peelings, to catch the squirrels. According to the "Little Brothers Raw Fur Sales Auction House" newsletter that we had subscribed to, coastal squirrel pelts were worth up to forty cents that year. I sent away for other free news sheets about the fur markets, so now there was mail coming directly to me in my own name. Before that, the only letters I ever received had come from my Grandmother. Talk about growing up fast.

From then on, other things in my life finally began falling into the right places. Sometimes this was by design and sometimes things just happened that way. Perhaps it was as Tom often tried to explain to me, that if a person wants a particular thing to happen, the best way to improve the odds is to continuously position your interests in the path that thing seems to frequent, and there will usually come a time when you and the thing you want will find reason to team up.

"And from there on it's all down hill," he assured me. Sometimes he took the subject a bit further and warned me, "For God's sake, don't ever get into a habit of quitting a project before you know for certain that it's not going to end in your favour. But on the other hand, you should always figure out ahead of time just exactly where that point is and make goddam sure that it's you that makes that decision and not somebody else." The different ways he tried explaining things like that to me often made my mind go fuzzy, but when he could build an example based around hunting and trapping, it became a lot more interesting and made more sense.

Our partnership turned out to be a profitable one, at least for me, because we began catching fur right from the second day on. Within a short time I was able to "run" my trapline alone, as Tom no longer had to accompany me to approve the trap sets or help with pressing down the stiff springs on the number one short-spring traps. He taught me how to set those traps on hard ground beside a log and use a three-foot stick as a lever to force the spring down. After a few clumsy attempts I got the hang of it and it worked just fine. I still use the method today with bigger traps. Within a couple of weeks I was even beginning to innovate my own style of trap sets, and by golly, they produced furs too.

Another thing that Tom had to teach me was the best ways to kill the animals in the traps. That can be a rather unsettling experience. I originally took it for granted that we would be shooting them with the .22, but Tom said, "No way." The muskrats that were not already dead had to be forced under water with a forked stick until they drowned, and the squirrels had to be strangled. Tom said these methods would prevent bruise marks on the hide side of the pelts that could reduce the money value by as much as half. I had already acquired a fondness for live squirrels, so these first dispatching jobs were not easy to do, but Tom taught me that a person simply must learn to numb his mind to such things. (The invention of the Conibear trap several years later was a godsend to both animals and trappers.) Tom did concede that when I caught a fox, we would use the .22 on it.

Along about the beginning of February I took my first fur shipment into Vancouver to sell. Because I did not have a licence, the furs could not be sold through the auction houses and had to be, as Dad described, "bootlegged" through a small fur buyer who paid cash with no questions asked. When I returned home with eight dollars and then compared the prices quoted in the auction house news sheet with the amount I was paid, there appeared to be about a 25 percent difference. Tom tried to argue that it was not such a bad deal under the circumstances. That theory was slow to sink into an unreceptive mind. It seemed to me it was some sort of a "cheat," and I could not understand why the buyer did it.

Dad tried explaining it a different way. "It's the price you pay for not doing things 'on the up and up.' If you had bought a licence, you could have sold those furs for ten dollars or more."

Well, maybe, but the licence would have cost ten dollars, so what would have been gained? At our dinner table we used to go "round and round" over subjects like that, and it took a while before it either made sense or perhaps I finally conceded to Dad's ominous warnings about prohibiting my venture if I didn't eventually buy a licence.

For Mom and Dad's benefit I made a big scene about putting four dollars back into the piggy. The other four dollars went into my pocket. Dad began a tirade about money then, as he suggested that I should have put six dollars into the piggy, just to prove that it was a profitable venture. The way I was doing it, no real profit had been made as I was only replacing the four dollars I spent on the traps. That was his opinion, but other plans had already been made and they took precedence. That other four dollars was used to buy more number one traps.

A positive spin-off from these dealings was that they made some of my arithmetic problems at school much clearer, like when the teacher was explaining the difference between investment, profit, and loss. Tom had a different take on this. "Figures are like poisonous snakes. If they can, they'll get you every time," he warned me.

Sometimes investments can be slow to recover though. In this case, I used most of my new number one traps to try for the foxes that left their tracks all over the fields when it snowed. Those foxes turned out to be a lot smarter than the muskrats were. As old Sourpuss Almont suggested one day when I was explaining my foxless woes to the boys, "You better get used to the fact that foxes are often smarter than some people are." Harry thought the remark was just hilarious, and that encouraged Almont to make a habit of dropping such verbal garbage in my presence whenever the opportunity presented itself. This always brought a laugh out of Harry, but he was a good laugher and it didn't take much to get him started.

Just the same, I did not appreciate Almont's suggestions, especially when I remembered that it was because of his scare story I was no longer allowed to carry the .22 pistol, which had almost become my hallmark. I could still use it, but not if I was alone, and there is a difference. I tried to persuade Tom to reconsider his decision and even showed him good reasons to do so. Now that I was an experienced tracker, I discovered there really were dangerous animals around, like bobcats and cougars. But when Tom came to confirm my suspicions he informed me the bobcat tracks were made by Dad's cocker spaniel and the cougar tracks had been made by a neighbour's German shepherd that was chasing deer, so I continued to be gunless on the trapline. He did console me a bit, though, as he promised that any time he or Harry was with me and we happened to see the deer chaser in action, I could tame him down with the 32.20. Tom further suggested that when we got him under control again, I could render him out like a wolf. Tanning its pelt would be a good learning experience for when I headed up north, and not only would the pelt look almost exactly like a wolf pelt, it would make just as good a bed cover too. Gunwise, that was the best deal I could get out of Tom at that time. It also put a time marker on that killer's life and as time went by, on a few other deer chasers as well.

There was no question that those foxes were smart, and I began experimenting with all of Tom's suggestions as well as trying some of my own bait concoctions, everything from chicken guts, pig guts, rabbit guts, and even sardines, but those foxes remained foxier than the trapper. Most of the time they would not even come close enough to my sets to steal the baits. Once in a while they actually did steal the bait without setting the trap off. A couple of times they went so far as to dig the trap out and tip it over without setting it off. Then, to add insult to injury, one of them had the gall to crap on the trap, again without setting it off.

When I reported this event to Tom, he concluded that this particular fox had probably been caught by somebody else before and had somehow escaped, so it was now what was known as a "trap wise" animal and would be much harder to catch than a normal one. He told me that a smart fox could be harder to catch than a wolverine, and wolverines were the trickiest animals and could do a trapper a lot more damage than just shitting on a trap. "You are goddam lucky not to have any wolverines around here, because those bastards can really complicate things," he warned or consoled me. But when I thought about that for a short moment, I came to a different conclusion. I figured if there were wolverines around Elgin it would make for a closed case in favour of my needing to carry the long barrel for self-defence. I began to wonder if Tom would know the difference between wolverine tracks and some big coon tracks in Barbara Lamb Creek, as he had already admitted he had never seen a coon track.

Those foxes may have thought that they were going to get away with their thievery forever, but I lay awake for nights on end, thinking and dreaming of devious ways to outfox them. So far, the bait that had come closest to producing a fox skin was sardines. I reasoned that if they liked little fishes, then bigger fish should be irresistible. With that in mind, I knew that Elgin Creek had what I needed. It was simple to borrow Dad's five-pronged hay fork and wade up the creek until I spotted a large, spawned-out dog salmon that made the mistake of thinking I could not see it hiding under a partly submerged log. When it was flipped out onto the bank, it turned out to be every bit as big as it had looked in the water. I was sure that no self-respecting fox would be able to resist such a meal. This fish probably weighed between twelve and fifteen pounds. It was too slimy and heavy to carry, so after finding a hooked stick to run through its gills, I dragged it most of the way back towards home, to a spot where Tom's field joined a neighbour's and there was a brushy patch where I had almost caught a fox earlier. As a matter of fact, the unsprung trap was still set there. After scratching out a hole big enough to hold the entire salmon, I reset the trap directly over top of it and covered the whole works with old dry leaves. Then I stepped back a few yards and admired my work. It was easy to see that from here on it was simply a matter of sitting back and outwaiting Mr. Fox's appetite. That could take a few days, but the set was close enough to home and the Elgin school that I could check it every morning and afternoon as I came and went from school.

It became a case of marking time, and to a kid my age, time went with the speed of cow molasses poured in winter. Not only that, but the inside of a school has to be the worst place to mark it from. I can still remember sitting in the Elgin school, staring out through the big windows in the direction that gold mine was going to appear from, daydreaming of how beautiful that fox pelt would look and of all the wonderful things that could be purchased with the money it was going to bring in. There were even warm thoughts of presenting my first fox skin to my mother so she could use it for a neckwarmer during the fierce Surrey winter. That would also keep it on display for the benefit of the rest of the world. Mom had a friend who used to come to visit and who had a red fox neckpiece that I admired for hours on end.

But Mom was not the sort of person who wore furs, so that scenario did not have to be dealt with seriously. That meant I could get back to thinking about the more worldly items I could turn the fox into, like a new fishing reel and perhaps even a bamboo rod to go with it. Up to then I was still using a cedar pole with a homemade wooden reel that did not work very well, especially when the fish on the end of the line weighed over a pound. A couple of larger fish had already cost me full-length lines as they made a fighting getaway, so there were good reasons to obtain better equipment.

I must have been in Grade 3 by then. I do not remember who the teacher was, but it was a typical one for those wartime years—female, not very bright, and above all, not understanding or even wanting to understand the priorities of manly things. She was continuously harping at kids for "not paying attention" to trivial things we were not interested in. She did teach us one thing though, and I'll bet you have noticed it by now too, and that is, there are few teachers who understand anything about the workings of the real world.

Hard, slow time or not, the truth is it took only to the afternoon of the third day, a Friday, one of the better days in a week, until the action began. On my way home from school that afternoon I decided to check out the fox trap before doing home chores and visiting The Shack. There was a large stump not far from the set that I had already chosen for an observation point so as not to leave fresh human scent too close to the trap. Well that day, lo and behold, there was movement in the grass by the set. Something had pulled the trap into the grass. So I had actually and finally outsmarted one and had him in a trap. Total elation!

But there was something about this animal that took me by surprise. Even though I could see part of the fox, it was not the orange-red colour I was expecting. This one appeared to be shiny black. Then it moved and I spotted the white tip on its tail, and bells rang deep in my mind to the point where my heart missed a beat or two. It dawned on me that my first fox was a SILVER! Talk about the height of luck. All sorts of things rushed through my mind, not the least of which was remembering the prices quoted in the most recent fur price lists. That year, silver foxes were selling for up to eighty dollars. EIGHTY DOLLARS! With that kind of money I could buy traps by the case. And there was a .22 rifle in a store in New Westminster that could be had for as little as fourteen dollars. With the connections Harry had, there would be no limit on the number of shells for it either. Perhaps there really was a benevolent God in Heaven and he had finally found me.

As soon as my senses came back down a little closer to earth, I realized there were a few problems that had to be solved right away. The first one was figuring out how to dispatch the fox. Any fool knows that you don't just walk up to a fox and strangle it like a squirrel or drown it like a muskrat. I was hesitant about getting too close to it at all, as Tom had warned me that a trapped animal will sometimes make one last super effort to lurch away from human approach and it can be enough for them to break loose. The obvious and earlier promised answer to this dilemma was hanging on the wall up at The Shack, which was only a fifteen-minute run away, but before going for the gun I wanted to get a peek at a real live silver fox.

As I jockeyed around a little bit to get a better look, the fox moved too and I began to realize my fox was not very large. My shadow mind suggested that the price of its pelt might not make the top bracket. Perhaps it was only a fifty-dollar fox. There was something else about it too. It was not jumping around the way I expected. Instead it kept curling up as if it wanted to go to sleep on top of the trap. It did not look as if it were dying, but it certainly was acting peculiar, and I couldn't figure out what was going on as there was too much tall grass obstructing the view. By then my curiosity was fully aroused, so I decided to move up a little closer to check on just how well the fox was caught—but not too close, as foxes have sharp teeth. Another of Tom's stories surfaced. This one was about how he once walked up to a snared wolf to give it a "good rap" in the head with the back of his axe. Just as he swung, the wolf jumped aside and broke the snare and as it ran past Tom it took a good loud snap at him but missed. Tom had drummed into me that I should NEVER let a wild animal bite me because it could result in catching rabies, or as he sometimes called it, "hydrophobia," which he assured me was not a nice catch to get. Old Tom was a good teacher and knew his subjects well and I was not the slowest student around, so we had a pretty good relationship that way. Some kids are just super lucky to be able to team up with a teacher like Tom Hasler.

As I warily walked up towards my fox, I saw that he did have a fine white tip on his tail, just like the ones in the animal picture books. But the closer I got to him, the more I saw that my fox was not just a small one but a *very* small one. Could there be such a thing as a ten-dollar silver fox? I sure hoped not.

When foxy realized I was approaching him, he raised his head and stared right at me and I saw there was something still more strange about him. This fox did not have the big ears and eyes that I was expecting to see, and his coat seemed to be spotted instead of having the beautiful frosty appearance that the picture books had shown. And this fox had a narrow head, small beady eyes, and almost no ears at all. Perhaps there were still a few things about silver foxes that Tom had forgotten to tell me yet.

About the time these questions were stumbling through my mind, foxy rose to his feet and I received a good clear whiff of him. I had prided myself on being a fast woodsy learner, and you can be assured that in the next fraction of a second I became a faster reactor. Three long jumps put me out of range. This was turning into a new and interesting experience because so far I had never met one of these on the live hoof either, but Dad had often warned me that when my time came I should not let one get closer than fifty feet. I did not know exactly how far a fifty-foot guess should be, but I gave this one the benefit of lots of doubt, which might have been more like a hundred feet. Whatever the distance was, it was enough.

We both stood there staring at each other. I have no way of knowing what was going through its mind, but in mine an eighty-dollar bill was floating away with the clouds. Probably the fifty-dollar and ten-dollar ones were too. I did remember that these animals were listed in the fur sales, so they were worth something, but they were always listed at the tail end of the newsletters so were surely worth nowhere near the value of a mink or fox.

There was still the original problem of clearing the trap without getting caught myself, and I knew the answer was sitting in his chair up at The Shack, so I lit out for there. On my way I stopped by my own house to dig out the latest fur sales report and sure enough, right down at the bottom of the last page was printed, “Skunks, top price $1.70 and lesser qualities at considerably less.” Like right down to forty cents. Well it wasn’t going to be a total loss because if it brought in the top price it would still amount to as much as two medium-sized muskrats. Just the same though, it was quite a comedown from the original eighty dollars and that new .22 from the store in town. Even if I received such an amount of money, that gun was not a certain acquisition because when I had broached the subject to Dad a few times, he informed me that I could not have a rifle of my own until I was older and more reliable, whatever that was supposed to mean. The way he expressed it made it sound a lot like "no." There was still another .22 closer to home. It was well used and could be had on the q.t. for five dollars, and I had been striving to acquire it without Dad's knowledge. I had already picked out the hollow stump I would keep it hidden in and was simply gathering the needed money that would clinch the deal. The dumb seller said he would not give credit on the sale, so it had to be cash-on-the-barrel-head or nothing. The needed five dollars was very slow to grow as it too had to be done on the q.t. and Dad was always snoopy about the things I spent my own money on. Like it was any of his business.

So now I was off to The Shack, not quite so fast although it was fast enough that I was unable to make out Mom's yodel that sounded something like, "Teddy, WATER." When I arrived at The Shack, still carrying the fur price list, I waved it at the three brothers as I blurted out what I had caught.

"You caught a WHAT?" Tom exclaimed. The other two just sat in their chairs and laughed until it looked like they might spill their drinks. As soon as we had all calmed down a bit, I showed the boys the price list and pointed out that this pelt was worth as much as two muskrats, but Tom just kept shaking his head and laughing as he explained to me, "Up north we never bothered with these things. They never were worth the time it takes to skin one, because you have to be damn careful how you do it. Come to think of it, I can't remember having skinned a skunk since I was about your age myself."

Almont piped up as he cackled, "Oh God, I remember that."

And Harry, he just sat there in his chair laughing until he was rocking back and forth, even though it was not a rocking-type chair. From the way they were all laughing and nodding their heads, they must have been remembering those wonderful days in the north country, the lucky dogs. Those good happy thoughts brought on enough reason for at least two full rounds of the UDL.

After the crew settled down a bit, I brought up the reason I was there. "Tom, now that I've got the skunk, how do I go about killing it so it can be skinned?"

Tom thought a moment and then reacted just exactly like I hoped he would as he nodded towards the guns that were standing and hanging behind my throne and said, "Put the stock on the .22 and go and shoot the damn thing right through the eye. Be sure to get close enough to make a perfect shot, because if you don't those crooked fur buyers, if they spot a hole in the pelt, will cheat you out of half its value." Tom then doled me out a single .22 short "Whiz Bang" cartridge, which I knew was the best kind because they came in a beautiful coloured box.

"Shouldn't I take along a couple of extras in case I miss?" I asked him.

"DON'T MISS!" Tom exclaimed. "And anyway, this way you won't be tempted to go grouse or pheasant hunting along the way, because we already have enough meat for all next week."

There seemed no point in challenging his decision, so rather than crowd my luck too far I accepted the single round, grabbed the pistol, and took off in a beeline to bag that foxy-skunk.

This was the first time I ever had to shoot an animal in a trap, and the first thing I learned was it's not all that easy to do, especially when it has to be shot through the eye. The animal seems to sense what's up and keeps its nose pointed straight at the executioner like it's daring you to do such a thing within the sight of God. In this case it didn't save the little stinker, as I had lots of time to get properly positioned and waited for it to calm down and turn its head sideways for the required "eye shot." It took only a few minutes of waiting and then this one died so fast it hardly even twitched. After waiting a few more safety minutes to be sure it really was dead, I walked over to see what a dollar-seventy animal looked like up close. Even after I unwired the trap and held everything at arm's length, it didn't look all that impressive and for sure it didn't look anywhere near as big as it had when it was standing on the trap with its tail cocked up.

Nevertheless, after making what seemed like a wise detour around our own house, it was back to The Shack with skunky, who was still locked into the trap, out on the end of a four-foot pole. The door to The Shack was open and I was about to parade my catch inside so the boys wouldn't have to get out of their chairs to admire it. Tom saw me coming and leaped to his feet faster than you can believe as he hollered at me, "DON'T YOU BRING

THAT GODDAM THING INTO HERE." He was so emphatic about it that he actually met me on the step where he spun me around, and his shove landed me thirty feet back out into the yard. He pointed to a stump that was another thirty feet away and instructed me, "Set it on that stump and I'll put my coat on and come out and show you how to skin that thing." So I handed him back the pistol and did as he instructed.

A few moments later the entire crew came out to admire skunky. Harry even remembered to bring along an almost-full bottle of UDL, and Tom was carrying a small kindling stick. Almont stood further off than the other two and from where he was grinning at me he asked, "You got any of the stuff on you yet?"

I had been real careful about this, so truthfully replied back, "Nope."

Tom was busy prodding the skunk around with his kindling stick as he commented, "I never seen one of these things that was spotted this way before."

Harry nodded his head in agreement as he added, "It ain't as pretty as the ones up north, either."

Almont, who was still laughing from a safe distance, added another five cents' worth as he informed all of us, "But it sure as hell smells about the same though." He sidled over a little closer, which resulted in another of his unneeded observations. "Hey, you missed its eyes by half an inch!"

Even though it was true, I had been hoping that nobody would notice or at least would have the decency to keep their trap shut. The bullet had actually hit just above and behind the eye and had come out in the same place on the opposite side of the head.

The next person to comment about it was my partner, as he assured all of us, "That's close enough. Ted will just tell the fur buyer that spotted skunks have four eyes, and the stupid bastard will never know the difference." Let me tell you, when a kid is lucky enough to have the type of partner I had, this world is at our mercy.

Tom was still forking the skunk around with his stick and he seemed to be in a bit of a quandary. He turned to me and said, "This is not a very big skunk, so it's not going to fetch you top price. Do you really want to be bothered skinning it? Skunks ain't easy to do."

At that, Harry and Almont began laughing harder than ever and I can remember Harry staggering around, slapping his thighs, until he made the mistake of doing it with the hand that held the bottle, which sent it bouncing along the ground. Luckily it was well capped and didn't break.

Well now, no self-respecting trapper is going to waste a fur animal just because it's small, and I informed the boys as such. Tom then nodded towards the skunk as he said, "Okay, but this time you are going to have to do it all yourself, because we ain't going to help you by holding it like we done with the rats." It was true that they had done that for me, but by now I had the experience of about ten muskrats behind me and as many squirrels. Tom was still nodding as he handed me his jack-knife, which was always sharper than mine was, and at the same time he rolled skunky over onto his back with the end of his stick. I was about to dig right in and get started by cutting the beginning line, which goes around the inside of the back legs, but Tom held me back as he used the stick to point to, and gently prod, a swollen area near the base of skunky's tail.

"You see that bulge?" Tom asked me.

"Yup," I replied in full confidence, eager to get started.

"Well that ain't a skunk's nuts. That's the scent gland that stores the spray, so when you cut down to that spot you got to cut around it. Now for God's sake be careful and don't cut into that sack or your mother will never let you into your house again. And if you DO slip, you sure as hell ain't staying here either. Now I MEAN it," Tom emphasized. By that time Harry and Almont had staggered over to another stump and plunked themselves down on it as they were having trouble getting the cap off the UDL. Those cowards.

The one thing I did notice about doing a skunk was that even without cutting into the sack, there is still a powerful odour about them. After I struggled with the job for an hour or so, however, it almost seemed to be wearing off because it wasn't as noticeable as it was when I started. As a matter of fact, it was becoming quite tolerable and I could not understand why the crew was leery of coming closer to the source. I could have finished the job faster if even one of them had come out and held skunky's back legs for me. Several times that afternoon the boys stuck their heads out of the door as they hollered over an inquiry, asking if I had gotten any of the stuff on me yet. Just the way they used the word "yet" made it sound like they were actually expecting it to happen. They seemed to have forgotten that they had already trained an expert.

Even though the smell was becoming pleasantly tolerable, it was still strong enough to notice, so I did remain wary and careful. It was difficult to tell where the smell was actually coming from as there were a few dribbles mixed into the fur, and that source is impossible to avoid. The entire problem became easy to ignore because once I got well started, the job became so interesting that the rest of the world and its values were temporarily set aside.

Tom was right about there being a difference between skinning muskrats and skunks. The pelt of a skunk does not peel off the carcass as easy as it does off a muskrat. The skunk was much tougher and I had to gently flay every inch of the hide away from the body. That made for slow, tedious work. Worth it though, because the experience gained on this one would make the next ones easier to do and was valuable training for my northern adventures, soon to come. When a person gets his face right down close to the working parts of a skunk, if there ever were any thoughts of becoming a doctor, lawyer, or engineer they just lose the race right there because skunks are every bit as interesting and you don't have to go to school for half a lifetime to learn to appreciate them.

The boys did come out once to offer some distant instructions, but it was a cool day and they soon drifted back into the comfort of The Shack. Not before they offered all sorts of descriptive advice and warnings about what would happen if I "nicked the sack" with the point of the knife. They really kept on about that. Even my partner seemed to be getting skeptical and he laughingly told me to take my time and do it right so Mom would not have reason to "run us both out of the country." I had never thought of that angle before, but it did raise thoughtful questions like, "What would it matter if she did? Because then Tom and I could simply go north together right now and he could teach me everything right there where it's all going to happen anyway." I have since heard tell that thoughts like that are called contemplation. In the 1940s our teachers called it "daydreaming."

It's hard to remember just how long it took to skin that skunk. The job was eventually finished, but it was not a particularly good one because I had nicked the hide in a few places with Tom's sharp knife that I wasn't used to using. As I finally straightened up from the job, I also could not ignore the fact that I had more of the stuff on me than I had earlier suspected. It didn't seem to be a lot more. Possibly nobody else would even notice it. Even if they did, the boys would be able to justify their laughs after all and I could simply clock it up to helping keep the party jolly. I knew there was a little on my hands as that was unavoidable, but this could be taken care of with Tom's supply of carbolic soap, which was strong enough to dissolve anything. The one thing that did have me a little worried was the possibility that a bit may have gotten onto my pants or jacket, as I had neglected to change clothes when coming home from school. Mom referred to this outfit I was wearing as my "school duds," and I had only about a set and a half.

I walked over to The Shack and lay the pelt on the outside woodpile, then opened the door, which revealed my partner sitting in his chair, whittling at a stretcher board that was being made to order for the skunk skin. After informing the crew that the skinning job was finished and the pelt was waiting for the stretcher, I stepped inside and plopped down in my usual chair beside the door, waiting for Tom to finish the board. Somebody said, "Close the goddam door!" which I did with my foot. It took only about one long moment before old Sourpuss Almont almost jumped out of his chair as he exclaimed, "Holy Christ!"

His reaction jolted everybody else up into a higher state too, and all three of the boys were staring straight at me. Strange looks on their faces too.

Tom came slowly up out of his chair and walked over closer to mine. He was gently shaking his head as he asked, "Did you prick the sack?"

My immediate answer was, "Oh no, I just got a little bit of the stuff on my hands from handling the hide and carcass, but it will wash off easy enough."

By then Tom was standing right over top of me and he used the same words again but a bit differently as he informed everybody, "You pricked the sack."

I was still sure that he was wrong, but it didn't help much when old Sourpuss confirmed, "He sure as hell did."

Harry never got out of his chair. He sat there rocking back and forth and laughed so hard that all he could say was, "Oh God, this is just like sixty years ago," which he repeated several times. If he was right, it made me wonder if some of the other wonderful things would begin repeating themselves also.

Tom and Almont didn't seem to be as impressed as Harry was, and as I stood up to reach for the stretcher, Tom threw the door open and slid my chair outside onto the step as he informed me, "I think you had better sit out here until you air off a bit."

"How long will it take?" I asked.

"Oh, not too long," my partner replied.

"Not over a month or so," old Sourpuss chimed in.

Harry just sat in his chair, rocking around, but had changed his comments to, "Oh God, oh God, oh God," even though I never considered him to be religious. Actually, none of the boys were unless you considered the opening of a bottle of rationed whisky on a Sunday afternoon as something divine.

I sensed that this eviction was not a particularly good turn of events, especially when Tom suggested that I start peeling off my clothes so we could figure out how many layers might be affected. They got me stripped right down to my shorts and I was getting goose-bumpy from the winter weather. About then Sourpuss came up with one of his brain waves, which was that perhaps I should have a complete bath with some damn strong soap. I had known all along that my hands needed a good washing but had never given any thought to an "all over" affair, especially not one with the type of soap I knew they had in mind. I was just about to say so when Tom nodded to Almont in agreement as he said, "That's a damn good idea." Just the way he made that statement warned me that my fate was sealed, which after a few other possibilities were discarded turned out to be all too true.

So I got the big tin washtub off the back wall of The Shack and Tom pointed out where to put it, right in the centre of the yard in front of The Shack and beside our big perching stump. We all pitched in by carrying hot water and a couple buckets of cold to fill the tub. Then out came a big, mean-looking floor brush, some towels, and a new bar of that yellow carbolic soap, all laid out on the stump beside the tub. Mom always claimed that this type of carbolic soap was made from 50 percent lye, and anybody that ever got the stuff in their eyes or into a cut or scrape would have to agree. It was so strong that I don't believe they make it any more. Tom also added a couple bars of stinky type soap as well. None of them offered to bring out a housecoat or heavy shirt, even though such things were hanging on the wall within sight of the tub. When I mentioned this, Tom informed me, "You ain't using any of my clothes, so you better get used to just toughing it out."

The toughing out part was not all that new. Living beside three creeks and a river, I had had the experience of unwanted outdoor baths before, but not quite the type that this one was shaping up to be. When everything was ready, I was waiting for the others to go back into The Shack and leave me to my own devices, but it wasn't going to be that way. I had never had a bath in front of three spectators before, and the way these ones were starting to roll their sleeves up it looked like they intended to help me out like Mom used to do when I was younger. I was not relishing this situation at all and could not understand why these old sourdoughs were making such a big event out of practically nothing. There was no question that they had the situation blown way out of need because I could hardly smell myself at all. But the way Tom nodded towards the bathtub, I knew, like it or not, this was the way it was going to be. So I peeled, climbed in, and squatted down.

We started out with the carbolic soap and the crew took turns with that floor brush until it cleaned me right off and my skin felt like a skinned onion looks. I was about to hop out of the tub and make a run for The Shack when old Sourpuss stuck his nose up close to me and stated, "I can still smell him."

Harry was standing back a ways and he nodded in agreement as he suggested, "I'll bet it's in his hair. Maybe we should shave him."

Tom was walking a circle around the tub at about a six-foot distance as he nodded and said, "Yeah, I think you're right, but I think we can fix him up without the scissors and it'll be done once and for all." He motioned me to stay in the tub, even though he must have noticed that I was shivering and rattling like a bare winter birch tree. He went into The Shack and within a couple of minutes was back with an armload of colourful bottles containing several brands of shaving lotion and two bottles of foul-smelling hair oil. He proceeded to pour a little from each into the tub, then stepped back as he told me to have one last good scrub in this new brew.

After Tom and Almont worked me twice over with that floor brush again, my skin looked like the skinned skunk carcass and felt like it was on fire. Just as I was finishing off in the tub, Almont reached over and poured the last of the two bottles of hair oil over my head, then stepped back as he told me to, "Rub it in real good."

After that I was allowed to make a run for The Shack where I dried off, warmed up, and put my clothes back on. The rest of them were busy hanging the tub up and bringing all the "ingredients" in. After everybody was inside, Tom began unthreading the top off a new bottle of UDL as he shook himself and commented, "By God, it's cold out there." From me, that hardly required an answer.

As I was putting the last of my clothes on and the crew was indulging in a good "swig-up," Harry walked close by me and then stopped and turned towards his brothers as he informed them, "You know, Ted smells like he just came out of a French Hoor House."

Almont started to laugh as he confirmed, "By God, he does." This brought out a big agreeable laugh from everybody. I wasn't sure if that meant it was a good smell or a bad one, but for safety's sake I laughed right along with the rest.

The general air in The Shack was on the rise. It began to feel like I was back among my peers again. Since it was a Friday evening, it was going to be steak night and I was hopeful as always on a Friday that I would be invited to partake. This turned out to be another of those dreams that never quite materializes. Things began falling apart as Tom was pouring a refill for everybody and wondered aloud, "I wonder what Fred and Avis will say about this?"

Old Sourpuss grinned in reply, "I'll bet it will be a while before Avis sends any more cakes or pies over to this Shack again. And all over a two-bit skunk too."

Tom chuckled in reply, "I guess we should have just thrown the damn thing into the river instead of fooling around with it."

That's when Sourpuss dropped another one of his bombs by suggesting, "You know Tom, if I was you I'd come over to my place for a few days, because you can't really tell how the kid's folks will take to all of this."

Tom stood there staring at Sourpuss for a moment and then nodded in agreement as he replied, "By God, that might be a damn good idea." He set his mug down and began filling a valise that he kept under his bed.

Harry watched him for a minute or so and then he got up and pulled a small suitcase out from under his bed and began doing the same as he muttered to all of us, "Be damned if I'm going to stay here and take the rap for everybody, so by God, I'm coming too. And anyway, a few days' leave from here should be enough to let this place air out a bit and perhaps some tempers next door."

All three of them thought that was just a hilarious statement, but I couldn't see any mirth in it at all because what they were about to do was commit complete desertion of their partner. Not only that, but I was facing a long, lonely, and steakless weekend.

While I glumly watched them load up the Hudson, they tried to console me by giving me the job of "keeping an eye on The Shack" until they decided to return. All the time I was watching them, I kept wondering how these rough Peace River bushmen could desert their partner in the face of such a trivial situation. When they piled into the car and it slowly started rolling towards the highway, Tom and Harry, who were sitting in the back seat, each holding onto a full bottle of UDL, waved them at me, which was their way of saying "So long partner."

Then it was my turn to go in the opposite direction, but it was with slower and sadder movement. It reminded me of one of Tom's favourite sayings, which he repeated many times, "When a man comes into this world, he arrives attached to his mother and among friends, but when he leaves, he goes out alone into an unknown and perhaps even unfriendly place." That afternoon I understood exactly what he meant.

It was almost dark when I arrived home. Mom was busy in the kitchen making supper, so I quietly passed her, heading for my bedroom where I intended to change into my work clothes. Mom barely glanced at me as I faded into the bedroom, except to suggest that it would be a good idea if I filled all the water buckets and wood box before dark and especially before Dad got home. I quickly agreed to do it all just as soon as I changed, and I really intended to as it seemed like a wise idea to prepare some safe ground in case unforeseen problems arose. Perhaps I made a mistake by not closing the bedroom door because just as I was pulling my second shoe off, I noticed Mom standing in the doorway, staring at me with a strange look on her face. After a long, silent, and breathless moment on my part, she finally asked, "What have you been into?"

Her wrinkled nose told me that there was no use neglecting to tell the truth, so I nonchalantly mentioned, "Oh, Tom was teaching me how to skin a three-dollar skunk, but I pricked the sack."

"Oh my God," Mom exclaimed. I expected the sky to start falling, but it turned out to be a sort of halfway affair as all she said was, "Well, get your clothes off and throw them out the window and then go hang them on the clothesline before Dad gets home. You can use the last of the hot water to have a bath, and as soon as you're finished, you get right down to the creek and start refilling everything."

I mentioned the baths I had already had at The Shack and also all the lotions that Tom had let me use. Mom just continued shaking her head as she laughingly told me, "I thought that was a strange-smelling skunk odour, but you are having another bath, regardless."

Things weren't turning out as badly as I had imagined they might, so I agreed to go through another indignity. As one last try to get out of it, I offered her the verdict from The Shack. "Harry says I smell just like a French Hoor House and Tom and Almont said so too."

Mom had been heading out the door as I said that, but she quickly turned back toward me with an astonished look on her face as she blurted out, "THEY SAID WHAT?"

I was just about to repeat it, but the look on Mom's face told me that it wasn't necessary. It dawned on me that I did not know what a "French Hoor House" was, so I made a mental note to inquire of some of the older kids at school. (Even though I hated that place, sometimes I had to grudgingly concede that a person could learn a few interesting things there.) When Mom heard

Harry's comment she dropped her cigarette, and as she stooped to retrieve it she seemed to be talking to the wall in a whisper as she commented, "That's probably the bunch that would know."

Mom did make me have that unnecessary bath, but this time I was allowed the customary luxury of having it beside the kitchen stove. This bath was not all that different from the ones at The Shack, because she added a whole bunch of ingredients to the brew too. This time they were things like baking spices. By the time I finished that bath I really could smell myself, and Dad's cocker spaniel, Lady, was giving me strange looks too. My body odour had been changed and that was for sure. Luckily Dad was late getting home that evening, so I had time to refill all the water buckets and the wood box to overfull before he arrived. Every time I entered the house with wood or water, Mom would pause at whatever she was doing and stare at me as she continued shaking her head.

It's amazing what a few drops of skunk juice can do for a person. After all the regular chores were done with a will, and just before the headlights of the Model A swung into our driveway, I had every schoolbook that could be found all laid out and opened on the dining room table. By the time Dad came through the back door I was so engrossed in arithmetic problems that had been hastily scribbled onto some paper that I never even noticed his arrival. He stopped in the kitchen long enough to give Mom a hug as she poured him a cup of coffee, which he then carried through the dining room, heading for his "big chair" in the front room. The unusual things he saw on the dining room table did cause him to slow down, but he only mumbled some inaudible comment as he shook his head. Disbelief, perhaps. He almost made it through the archway into the front room, but then he stopped dead in his tracks and exclaimed, obviously to me, "Get that damn dog out of here."

I did not catch on fast enough, not that it would have mattered in the longer term, but replied, "Lady is out on the porch."

At that, Dad got a puzzled look on his face and backed up a couple of steps so he could glance under the table where Lady often kept herself out of sight. When he saw she wasn't there, he began looking around the room with that quizzical look until he zeroed right in on me. By this time Mom was standing in the doorway between the kitchen and dining room, watching, but not saying a word.

I cannot describe the look that came onto Dad's face about then, but it sure was different from his normal appearance. He set his cup down on the table and seemed to be making a slow, deliberate, mental decision that resulted in his arm coming up to point at the outside door as he said in the most authoritative voice I had ever heard him use, "GET OUTSIDE."

Under circumstances like that, no kid offers argument. Without a word I grabbed my jacket as fast as humanly possible and made myself scarce through that door. Once outside, my second-best friend jumped up and offered condolences, and after a few mutual hugs and slurps she let me share her bed with her. I gratefully accepted the invitation. Lady had been through ordeals similar to this herself for almost the exact same reasons, so we had a great deal in common. It's times like that when a person learns to appreciate the value of true and loyal friends.

It was cold and dark, and I was getting mighty hungry before Mom opened the back door and quietly said, "You had better come inside because you can't live out here."

I wished there was some way I could refuse the offer, but I could not come up with any answer other than to ask Mom, "Can Lady come in too?"

"I guess so," she replied, "because she sure smells better than you do."

We both quietly entered the house and Lady snuck straight to her favourite spot under the table. I was beginning to think about joining her when Dad nodded towards a chair beside the heater. As I sat down, I noticed that there was something different in the house. It was the smell. And it wasn't from me either. I sat there trying to be as inconspicuous as possible while Dad looked at me and began sprinkling something onto the heater. He referred to it as "incense," but it was almost the same ingredients as Mom had put into my bath water a couple of hours earlier. The ones I can remember were cinnamon, garlic, and curry, but there were others. When they were scorched on top of the stove that way, they made the house smell like "bake days," but not quite the same. You can take my word for it, the aroma from heated garlic and curry does not mix well with cinnamon and sugar.

Dad never said anything threatening to me directly, but as he sat there experimenting with his incense ingredients he mused aloud about all the things that should happen to "those goddam bastards who live at The Shack." The mental tension in the house became so thick and heavy that Lady came out from under the table and hopped up onto my lap, something she rarely tried to do as she had been taught not to. Nobody told her to get down, so she stayed there a while and every time Dad sprinkled more of his "goodies" onto the heater, she would tense a bit. Pretty soon she had me doing it too. As we both sat there trying to console each other, I can still remember coming up with the thought that there were things in this world that smelled worse than skunks.

As the old saying reminds us, there is a limit to how low things can sink before there is no other direction but up, and that's about the way that weekend went. For two solid days I worked on the end of a five-foot crosscut saw until we had a stack of wood bigger than any of us could remember having before. It was all done voluntarily too. The weekend finally came to an end and never before in my life had I been so happy to go to school on a Monday morning. It was like an escape.

I was going to a one-room school at Elgin, where a single teacher taught Grades 1 to 6. At this time I must have been in Grade 3 or 4, which even in that school was not the most prestigious level of learning, but that morning saw me elevated to the position of most popular kid on the playground. Up to that time, none of the girls had ever shown me much positive attention, but that day things changed fast. They began making great displays of noticing me and would very deliberately come up close, then with a squeal of delight would run off holding their noses. And of course the boys were as curious and envious as you can imagine.

When the teacher came out onto the school porch and rang the handbell, we all lined up outside and below the steps while one of the older kids, usually a Hadden, raised the flag. Then the teacher trooped us all inside, smallest ones first and tallest last, so I was able to get a few more moments of freedom than most of the rest. This particular teacher would hang back behind the last kid like she was herding us through the door, as if she expected or hoped one of us would try making a run for it. I never did see anybody try it, but just to show off her determination, after the last kid had passed through those double doors she would make a great scene of slamming them shut and driving the bolt home. She told us that the bolt was to keep the doors from rattling in the wind, which would be a distraction to the classes, but we knew better. Some of us suspected that she had received her training at the Reform School in Surrey, which was not far away. In those days all kids, especially boys, were continuously made aware of what and where it was and of all the different avenues that could lead into it. Some of the stories we were told about that place sure made it sound interesting, but it was one of the few places of interest that were not quite interesting enough for us to want to find out about first hand.

On this particular day I did note that the teacher was following extremely close behind me, even though I had not made the slightest attempt to cut and run or, for that matter, do anything out of the ordinary. She was so close to me, in fact, that I deliberately made an equal show of marching briskly straight to my desk, but she followed right on my heels. Obviously something ominous was up, but I couldn't for the life of me figure out what might be bugging her unless another kid had framed me for some deed. This had been known to happen.

Before any serious guessing became necessary, the teacher sidled around me about an aisle's width away, and with a puzzled look on her face she asked me what I believe is the stock female schoolteacher's question, "And what have you been into?"

This time I wasn't a bit worried about telling the truth. In fact I relished the opportunity, as this time I was on completely legal grounds. Everything had happened after school, away from school, and on private property, which meant it was no business of hers. To keep the discussion on a sociable level, however, I never bothered to inform her of such legalities and instead gave her the full rendition of the story, which started out with, "My partner, Tom Hasler, was teaching me how to skin a five-dollar skunk, but I slipped and pricked the sack with the knife."

As she began digesting that information, she was shuffling back another yard or so away from me, shaking her head and mumbling something that sounded like, "Oh, wouldn't you know it." In earlier discussions with me she had been well informed about who and what my partner was. I knew there was no other kid in the school or even in the district who could claim to have a real, honest-to-goodness, adult partner of the type I had. That made me noticeably different, and I used every excuse to make sure that everyone else knew and understood it. Popularity can be a good ego builder. Every kid needs at least a little bit of it and there are some who indulge to the limits.

It sure is a wonderful feeling to be able to sit in front of a teacher and know it's you that's right for a change. Everything was going my way and some of the other kids were beginning to show signs of awe and envy at my popularity. About then the teacher came to a decision and told me, "Well, Teddy, you are finally going to get your wish because it's to the back of the room for you. *All the way back*." She walked to the back of the room and showed me exactly how far back she meant. We relocated my desk right beside the door, which put me as far away from her desk as I could be and still be in the room. This suited me just fine. If a kid had to go to school, then a seat like that had to be prestige in itself.

All went well for most of the morning, and the teacher even allowed us to open a window. I moved my desk closer to that window, both for the benefit of the others and also for my personal view of the bushland that came right up to the schoolyard. Some days you could see the most interesting things out there—the odd deer, sometimes with a dog or a pack of them chasing it, and even some good, all-round dogfights that were always worth watching. Those fights often divided the school, with some kids wanting to break it up and others, who had their favourite dog in there, goading it on, especially if their dog happened to be winning. A few times when a dogfight was going loud and strong, even the teacher would become hyped up, usually on the side that wanted to break the fight up. She would send a couple of the older boys out to do exactly that, so of course all the rest of the kids would rush to the windows to watch how everything went. The honest fact was the dogs hardly ever hurt each other and it was always a great way to knock twenty to thirty minutes out of a school day.

But as this morning progressed, the older boys, just to make themselves noticed, started getting up and opening more windows. This went on until some cream puff complained about being cold. Everything was fine for me until the teacher came back to my desk and stood there staring at me till I felt uncomfortable. Finally she made an astounding decision. “Teddy, the rest of us are not going to put up with this any longer. You are going home until that smell wears off of you.”

The complete implication did not sink in right away, so I asked, “How long will it take?”

She answered, “I have no idea, but I'll send a note home to your mother explaining the problem and maybe she will know of something that can make you more bearable to live around.”

By this time I recognized what her decision meant and remembered what Almont had said about this stuff taking a month or so to wear off. I kept my mouth shut and even tried to look depressed, but my mind was spinning into space from the realization of what she was offering me. I was almost breathless in anticipation, both in fear she might come to her senses too soon and see that she was offering me another midwinter holiday and in ecstasy at my own realization of the same thing. This was right in the middle of the trapping season, and Tom had already told me it was the time of year when the foxes mate and do other stupid things that make them easier to trap.

That teacher did not have to repeat her travelling orders. I immediately shoved everything down into the bottom of my desk and by the time she handed me that unnecessary “note to home,” I had my coat on and was ready and willing to obey orders. I was in such a hurry to get out that there was no time even to say “So long” to my best friends. As the teacher slammed and rebolted the door behind me, I cleared the steps in one bound, the fence in another, and was out of sight of that place before she could change her mind and verbally stop me or move fast enough to catch me.

Did you ever notice when you went to school how it was that some kids seemed to have all the luck? Well it used to be that way back in the 1940s too, especially at the Elgin school, and this reminded me of an interesting thing that happened not long before I went there. That was a time when Elgin still had some of its characters. There was a part-time logger who lived up the hill about a mile from the Elgin school and who went under the name of Joe Bush, though he was known to most of us as “Old Dirty Shirt.” The reason for that name, so the adults told us, was because he changed his shirt only once a year whether it needed it or not. One day Joe arrived at the school with a big rope slung over his shoulder and an already-tied-in hangman's noose at one end of it. Joe was angry. Somebody had opened his front pasture gate and his milk cow had gotten away, and he suspected the culprits were hiding in the school. As the story went, Old Dirty Shirt ordered everybody out into the yard, teacher included. Then he slung the rope up over a strong branch of a chestnut tree and told the group that if the culprits were not pointed out, he was going to begin hanging everybody, again teacher included. The teacher went into hysterics. About that time a neighbour came by and talked Joe out of stretching any necks, and things were somehow resolved more peaceably. I do not believe they bothered to involve the police, but it was the talk of the community for a long time afterwards. Perhaps it still is. Every time I heard somebody tell of that event, it made me think of the truth in the statement "It's always the other kids that have all the luck." In the five years I went to that school and the three more over at Semiahmoo in White Rock, not Old Dirty Shirt nor anybody else ever came to offer to hang a teacher.

But in my own less exciting case, when I arrived home and blurted out the wonderful news to Mom, she turned out to be not nearly as enthused about this event as I had hoped she would be. When Dad came home it became downright sticky. I almost dropped through the floor when he announced that if I was not going to be allowed into school, it was time I learned to make myself more useful at home, like paying for my keep by working on the woodpile until the woodshed was full (and we had a big one). We had a long three-way discussion about that. It ended up in a compromise agreement. I would spend the mornings on the woodpile, but the afternoons would belong to me. It was left unsaid, but we knew that meant out in the fields and up the river and creeks. Somehow we were able to avoid mentioning Old Tom's Shack. There was another condition I had to agree to and that was NO MORE SKUNKS. This turned out to be not such a bad agreement as Dad got his woodpile, which kept him happy for a long time, while I was able to stretch the perfume odour into ten wonderful winter days on the trapline that netted me a dozen muskrats and several squirrels. By the time the freedom smell had worn off and I returned to that hard desk, I was the richest kid in the school.

The only really negative thing that came out of the ordeal was the final fate of the foxy-skunk. The folks would not allow me to bring the stretched pelt into my bedroom where it could have dried much better and faster, so I had to leave it out in the woodshed, hanging on the wall. The truth that there had to be more than a few drops of scent on the pelt was often driven home to us as even from out in the woodshed, when the wind was right, everybody in the house was reminded that the pelt was out there. One evening when I returned home from a visit to The Shack, I went into the woodshed to check on how well the pelt was drying and discovered that pelt and stretcher board were gone. I ran into the house to make inquiries of Dad, who was reading the paper in his "big chair," but he said he knew nothing about it other than when he arrived home there was a pack of dogs in the yard, led by a big German shepherd, and they may have grabbed it and run. "These Elgin dogs have a bad reputation for chasing and tangling with skunks, you know," he reminded me. This was a fact that anybody around the area who owned a dog could not deny. That German shepherd was aging faster than he could have suspected. So that was what happened to my first six-dollar skunk.

With Tom's enlightened style of teaching I soon became as proficient a trapper and hunter as the resources of the area would allow, and it did put money into my pocket that would have been harder to come by in any other way. My trapping ability became good enough that my reputation spread from White Rock to Crescent Beach and all the way up the rivers to the edge of Langley, all within only a couple of years. I was often astounded when perfect strangers, mostly adults, from all over the district came to our house wanting to speak to me specifically. Did things like that happen to you when you were ten? Most of those people were trying to locate their missing dogs and cats. Of course I seldom knew anything about these animals, but I was always most willing to keep my eye open for them and report back to the owners if they were ever seen. Some of those conversations were invigorating. Talk about becoming a popular kid! As I remember, Mom and Dad always refused to become involved in those discussions, so I was having to learn at an earlier age than normal how to verbally defend myself and especially my business.

It was about two years after the first episode that I had another unintentional experience with a skunk. This time it was not one of those little spotted types but a big hooded skunk, a real "pretty-boy." This fellow had also been caught in a trap intended for a fox, and its behaviour was different from what I expected. I was two years older than I had been before, and that made me quite a bit bolder, so this time I walked right up to the fifty-foot safety margin for a good close examination. The skunk responded like he wanted to be friendly and perhaps even forgiving, as he never tried lurching away or threatening me with his "works." For several moments we stood there looking each other over out of curiosity. This seemed strange as all my experiences so far had taught me that wild animals, when they are cornered or trapped, act just as wild as you would expect. And there was no trace of odour either. More strange.

It occurred to me that I might have caught somebody's deodorized pet. I knew that none of our close neighbours had such an animal, so it was easy to assume that this fellow must have come from quite a ways off. Perhaps it was like those house cats that city people often brought out near the farms to turn loose so they could help the farmers keep control of the mice in their barns. What usually happened was the home-grown barn cats that the farmer already had would never let those city slickers into their barns, so the city cats ended up having to fend for themselves out in the fields and bushland, just like wild cats, which the survivors quickly became. The survival rate among them was not particularly high, at least not in our neighbourhood, as Tom had already taught me these cats will become the most proficient pheasant poachers in the world, way worse than any kid with a .22. They were much worse than a mink because with their domestic background they were wise and bold enough not to be put off by human scent. Tom did not like these cats around his farm, so we often did control work on them. This was one of the few issues that Tom and Dad were in agreement on because those same cats, before they discovered pheasant nests, usually trained on domestic rabbits and chickens first. They also had a habit of messing up my mink and fox trap sets, so those wild domestic cats acquired very few human friends throughout the area and were dealt with accordingly.

However, if this skunk was of the domesticated variety, it had not yet reverted to the wild, so it was an easy decision to spare its life and bring it back to human persuasion again. The skunk looked so sleek and cuddly that it was easy to daydream of having a fine and interesting new pet. There was another thought lurking in the back of my mind also. I had recently read that deodorized skunks were worth a great deal of money, like up in the fifty-dollar range, so this catch could represent the equivalent of two mink. If I were to sell it as pet, there would not be the chore of having to skin it either. Whichever way I decided to go, I was about to become VERY rich. Either mentally or physically. If I decided to go the money route, that hot little .22 cached out in the bush was becoming a real possibility again.

The skunk was acting so tame and friendly that I had an urge to go right up and pet it, but decided to wait until it was inside a sack or building. There was a good possibility that once freed from the trap, it might not be as tame as it was now implying. Also, it was caught only by the ends of two toes, which meant that if I was not careful enough it could spook into making a lurch for freedom and perhaps even slip out of the trap.

By the time of this skunk episode I had become proficient at letting animals out of traps without hurting them beyond what they and the trap had already done to themselves. I occasionally had to release pets that were owned by our close and known neighbours. The method that worked best was to approach the animal slowly and quietly with one of the big, heavy, coal sacks we used to buy lump coal in. The sack for this job had a drawstring woven around the top opening. As soon as I dropped it over top of the animal, I would pull the drawstring tight around both the animal and the trap. Those sacks were thick enough that no animal could bite through them, so while it was overwhelmed I would feel through the sack and locate the trap, then force the spring down enough that the animal could pull free. A large dog was not so easy. I had to get the sack over its head and make sure the drawstring was snugly tied, then cut the snare or step on the trap spring. Before the dog knew it was free, I had to loosen the drawstring on the sack and jump well back as the dog shook off the sack. If it was a large dog, that could be a dicey moment. Tom taught me that it was wise to get well out of its way, even to the point of climbing a tree, because some dogs were slow to understand the difference between liberators and tormentors and were not too forgiving when they suffered indignities to their pride.

After all these thoughts had spun through my mind a few times, I ran home and grabbed the coal sack and returned to collect the bonanza. I was just about to throw the sack over Pretty-Boy's head (I had already decided on his name) when I realized that in my excitement I had picked up the wrong sack. This one did not have a drawstring in it. That was no real problem because coal sacks were large and made of heavy jute and there would be no problem keeping even a skunk as big as this one in the sack. When he was free from the trap I would simply twist the top closed and carry him the short distance to home, where I would release him inside a building, probably in my bedroom, so I could get a good evaluation of how tame he really was.

There was no trouble getting Pretty-Boy into the sack. He even seemed to appreciate the darkness as he voluntarily crawled right down to the bottom of it. Things were looking better all the time, as it was obvious somebody had trained this skunk well. This would make him that much easier to sell. I untied the wire that fastened the trap to the drag. The next thing was to release his foot, so I felt around from the outside and soon had a good grip on the trap, but as the sack was thick and the trap was a stiff number one, my hands were not strong enough to compress the spring. That was no problem because Pretty-Boy was so co-operative that he was not struggling at all. So I stood up, got the trap positioned to what I thought was just right, then used my foot to press down on the spring. That worked perfectly and I could feel and see by movement that Pretty-Boy had jumped free of the trap. When I stepped down on the trap I must have pinched his toes or something, because he let out a small squeak, but things like that have to be expected.

I reached down to roll up the sacked skunk—and what came up through the sack but IT. Not the skunk, but the smell I thought he didn't have. In a lot faster time than it takes to write or tell, I had leaped back to the fifty-foot safety mark again. Oh, that little stinker! A moment or two later, Pretty-Boy stuck his nose out of the sack, took a long look at me, and nonchalantly ambled across the trail into a patch of salmonberries. He was hardly even limping.

Now another worry presented itself and that was that some of the stuff was on me. It was not as strong as I remembered from the spotted skunk ordeal, but it was still strong enough that there was going to be no way to fool my folks. This was an addition to my education though, as I learned the stuff was strong enough to go through a thick coal sack and still do damage. Amazing!

It's hard to remember if I was more angry or amused about the outcome of that event. I couldn't conjure up bad thoughts towards Pretty-Boy as he was so pretty and friendly and acted like he wanted to be cuddly. It was a great mental letdown to lose him. And after the reality of another fur fortune's escaping me had sunk in, I was homeward bound to face the repercussions of still being attached to a family. Times were beginning to change around our house, though, and Mom and Dad seemed to be getting used to strange ideas, happenings, and smells. It was no later than my twelfth birthday that they pretty well tossed in the towel as far as trying to make me see the world through what they called "conventional eyes." Even this latest skunk accident raised only quiet head shakings from them. They were learning to share my enthusiasms, especially when I did finally start bringing home some of those foxes and mink.

As it turned out, those two skunks were the only ones that ever "got" me. Pretty-Boy didn't do as good a job as the spotted one either, as all he got for me was four days away from school. Ever since then, whenever I catch a whiff of skunk out in the bush it immediately reminds me of those days of long ago, when schools, teachers, and skunks were so entwined because they all had a profound effect on shaping my life. For better or worse, who can say? But one of them still brings back fond memories. Ah, the smell of freedom!

CHAPTER 3

GAME WARDENS

Down in Surrey during the 1940s and perhaps even before, there lived a man whose name was the terror of every farm boy who owned a gun. His name was Old Pike and he was the Game Warden. I never had the opportunity to meet or know him and did everything in my power to keep our relationship that way. Come to think of it, I can't remember what he was supposed to look like or what type of vehicle he was said to drive. Probably he would be easy to recognize because of the dark cloud that followed him and his reputation everywhere.

You should not laugh at that description because I'll bet either one of us would recognize the Devil in a moment, even if we hadn't met him yet, and to young gun-toting boys, Game Wardens were pretty well in the same league. The stories handed down to me by the Lewis brothers, Doug and Lloyd, and later on by Don Turnbull and the MacBeth brothers, who were all hunting sages in the district, were enough to keep the hair curled on any kid who aspired to become a hunter. Every story passed down had heavy ominous overtones to it, and when these were told and retold, confirmed and reconfirmed at every opportunity, it did have an effect on young kids. Whenever and however the stories were passed down, Old Pike was always portrayed as the Joker in a card game or a phantom that could leap out of the bush. Even the word "Warden" has a repressive sound to it. When you think about it, there are Prison Wardens, Park Wardens, Block Wardens,

Forest Wardens, and then these Game Wardens, and every one of them has been delegated authority to impose and enforce "Thou Shalt Not"-type rules. Just try to think of one positive thing that any type of Warden ever did for you. It's much easier to remember all the things they have done *to* you. Thoughts like these are infectious, especially among the hunting fraternity. My instructors said the warden always had to be considered, and their stories and attitudes about him had considerable influence on this kid's growing pains.

It was not that I considered myself a poacher or those other things Dad used to refer to as crooks and shysters, but the stories did imply there were some rather vague rules that governed hunting. It was also obvious that my mentors had almost schizophrenic interpretations of them, so it was often left to juvenile opinion to decide what the real rules were. This started me questioning everything and everybody around me, and many adults, especially teachers, did not take kindly to being continuously contradicted by a younger expert. Permit me to offer a hypothetical example of how easy it is to get drawn in to this questioning.

Let's say an adult hunter (the Elder) has taken a young protege (the Younger) out for an evening duck hunt. The two hunters have stayed out on the mud flats right to the legal end of a shooting day, which has always been posted as one hour after sunset. No problem here yet, as they have bagged well under their limit. The Elder says they have to comply with the law and head for home. And anyway, it was damn cold out there that evening. It is really slow going what with the muddy slipping and stumbling in the fading light, and it is the best part of a mile back to their truck, which will take close to an hour. When they are almost back to the vehicle, the light has fallen below not only legal limits but probably safe ones too, but even so there is that twilight period when we can still see things against bright water and fading sky. These two saintly nimrods round the last bend in the irrigation ditch and lo and behold, not over thirty yards ahead of them rests a large flock of mallard ducks. As you probably know, ducks don't see any better at that time of evening than we do, so the damn fools just sit there quacking and squabbling about who knows what. Ducks in the dark are no smarter than you are.

Now is the time for decisions. What would you do under those circumstances? Well, that's exactly what these hunters do too. The Elder steps safely aside as he raises his shotgun and hoarsely whispers to his companion, "This shot will make them rise, so get ready to give them both barrels." Everything goes exactly to spoken and unspoken plans. As the ducks rise up on a hundred pairs of wings, four more shots fill the sky with feathers and the ditch with dead and dying ducks.

The instructor is in full command of the situation as he orders the novice, "Get down there into the ditch and start throwing the ducks up onto the bank while I stay up here and watch for flashlights." He never mentions whose flashlight he is referring to, and the protege does as he is told. As the wounded birds have their necks wrung, they are added to the pile that did not need the operation. Then the Younger crawls up onto the bank himself. He is about to pull off his water-filled boots to drain them when the Elder growls, "Are you going to sit there until that bastard comes and hauls you off to the penitentiary? For Christ sake, smarten up and start hauling these things to the truck." It was done without any more words being said.

As the ducks are thrown into the back of the truck, the learner silently counts the bag. He turns to the leader and quietly informs him, "We got eight too many ducks."

The instructor replies, "By God, we do. Well, we sure as hell aren't going to leave them here, so we'll stuff nine of them behind the seat. If we are checked, we'll claim that we are still one short of the full limit and that will deflect that son-of-a-bitch from any further nosing around." That's the way it was done and the drive home was uneventful as the phantom from the fog never did step out with his red light.

During the following few days the ducks are all duly plucked and cleaned and some are distributed to other needy mouths that are hungry enough not to ask embarrassing questions, so the law is never the wiser and as the instructor informs the pupil, "When the law does not know something, then no law has been broken." That's the way it is taught, and it is taught at an early enough time that the Younger does not challenge his elders. Not unless he wanted a fat lip or to be left home from the next excursion, he didn't. Anyway, the theory is backed up by some being taught at school like, for instance, the Younger can remember a teacher explaining to a class that when a tree falls in the forest and there is no human ear there to hear it, no noise was made.

So there you are. As you can see, this situation and its legality or morality can be used as a ruler for all sorts of other situations. In this case, what should have been done and at what point? Who really draws the lines between pure white, shades of grey, and things darker? As people get older, they spend a lot of time contemplating things like that.

As it turned out, the first Game Warden I ever met had a lot to do with setting me on my life's course, even though at the time our relationship kept me on a seesaw mental state for a while. Tom Hasler arrived at Elgin about mid-1943 and it must have been shortly after that the old Game Warden (Pike) was replaced by a new fellow by the name of Hughes who lived on the northern edge of Cloverdale. I do not remember what happened to Pike but assume that he retired or went on to wherever it is that old Game Wardens go. By the time I met Hughes I already had about two years of grounding in the philosophy of the Hasler brothers.

Believe it or not, my first meeting with Hughes was a deliberate affair set up by me. It must have been 1946 or 1947, by which time I already had considerable experience with midnight trapping. I decided that it was time to come out into the daylight and buy a trapping licence. This was only partially because of conscience, but mostly because by not having a licence I had to sell my furs through those under-the-table deals with small independent buyers who were able to slip my pelts in with someone else's. It all had to do with figures and paperwork and it reminded me of what Tom had said about how the venom from some poisonous snakes can result in slow death. The midnight deals had worked out okay, except for that fact that the independents always paid on the low end of what the auction houses did, but with a licence I would be able to cover the cost of the licence and also make a larger profit by expanding my operations beyond Tom's private property. With my new knowledge I had begun spotting out more quiet green areas.

So sometime in the early fall, with money in my pocket, I informed the rest of our crew what I was about to do. They all listened to me in silence and then one by one came down the cautionary verdicts.

From Tom, "You be damn careful not to tell that goddam Game Warden of what you have been doing for the past three years, and absolutely don't you tell him nothing about us packing these rifles and pistols around or about us plugging the odd deer now and then. When dealing with those kind of bastards it's best to just tell him what you have to, like your name, address, plunk down your money, and keep your mouth shut as much as possible. And then as soon as he hands you the licence, get the hell away from him just as fast as you can and STAY AWAY!"

Harry put the finishing touches to the instructions with, "Yeah, some of those bastards are worse than cops and will even pinch their own grandmothers."

It was with considerable apprehension that I parked my bike outside the Game Warden's front gate. I can't remember what it was I expected to encounter when I knocked on the door, perhaps someone in uniform or a big scowling brute with a black eyepatch, but the fellow who answered my knock was none of those things. He was an older man of medium build and he had an authoritative or military air about him. That was not particularly intimidating to me as we had grown up around many military people who retired to the White Rock area and were still addressed as "Captain," "Major," or "Colonel" this and that, even though the wars they fought had ended long ago. They were mostly World War One types, but there were a few Boer War veterans too. I do not remember anybody being addressed as "General." We had been told that all of those types retired over near Victoria

This fellow was obviously the Game Warden, and when I told him why I was there and what I wanted, he politely nodded his head as he shook hands with me and said with a slight English accent, "I'm Hughes. Come on in." I slotted him as ex-British army.

The Game Warden nodded to a chair beside his desk, so I sat down and he opened the conversation. "How old are you Ted?"

"I'm almost twelve, sir."

He stared at me for a moment or so before he continued with, "Have you ever done any trapping?"

"No sir, but I have three friends from the Peace River country who are going to teach me as soon as I buy a licence. They are three brothers named Tom, Harry, and Almont Hasler, and they have trapped all over the north country," I informed him.

"You don't say?" the Game Warden replied with an odd look and perhaps a brighter twinkle in his eyes. "It just so happens that I've spent considerable time up in the north myself."

I was just about to ask him if he knew the boys at The Shack when Tom and Harry's instructions resurfaced in my mind and I began sliding into a bit of a sweat, which was not relieved when the Game Warden seemed to speak to the ceiling as he quietly murmured, "So the Hasler brothers have retired down here, have they?"

I didn't know if the question was directed at me or not, so I just sat there nodding my head and kept my mouth shut.

The Game Warden seemed to be reminiscing as he continued, "But when I was up there, I wasn't with the Game Department. I was still in the provincial police."

Oh God. My heart, stomach, lungs, and everything were beginning to slide downwards again and the inside of my mouth felt and tasted like burned toast. It would not have been so bad if the Game Warden didn't have that way of seeming to stare right into the centre of my head. At that moment I would have willingly paid anybody a silver dollar to instill in me the courage to jump up and run out the door. But the heat in that room kept me frozen to the chair.

After a silent moment or two, Hughes broke the spell as he said to me, "I'm sorry Ted, but I cannot sell you a trapping licence unless one of your parents comes over here to sign it for you. It's because of your age, you see, and the problem is, a licence to trap is also a licence to carry firearms, and you are not allowed to do that until age eighteen. These licences are actually called Special Firearms Licences. And do you know that they cost ten dollars per year?"

I already knew about the atrocious price of the thing, and he showed me a book of them that had the price right up there in the corner, so I silently nodded acknowledgment. He had another surprise for me when he pulled from his drawer a sheet of yellow stickers and told me one of them would have to be stuck to the back of my licence when I got it. The writing on the sticker said "the bearer" was a minor and must be accompanied by an adult any time the bearer was bearing firearms. All of this stuff was news to me and I did not deem it to be good news either.

When our short business was over and I had informed the Game Warden that I'd get my Dad to come in the next time he came over to the Surrey Co-Op to buy feed, we drifted into more amiable conversation. Hughes must have had nothing else to do that day, as we spent the next hour or so trading stories. His were about experiences in the north country and the Okanagan and mine were of all the things I thought I knew about the people around Elgin. I soon noticed some strange things about the Game Warden's stories of the north country. Even though some of them were about the same places and events the Haslers had talked about, these new stories seemed to have a different slant to them. Just the same, the Game Warden's versions were fascinating too, and they reconfirmed some of Tom's observations, which in turn helped to prove that some of Dad's doubts were misplaced. It was possible that the Haslers, because they were getting old, had simply forgotten some of the nitty-gritty details that didn't really matter anyway. And even the Game Warden looked old enough that his memory could have been slipping a bit. A listener has to take all this into account and then piece together his own conclusions.

Hugh Hughes and I hit it off well and I even loosened up enough to repeat some of the Hasler stories to him. He seemed to get a great kick out of them and after listening to a couple, he became so enthused that he sat and laughed and slapped the desk or his thigh as he exclaimed, "So that's the way it was, was it?" Hughes had some good stories to lay back onto me, and I made a mental note to remember some that I was sure the boys at The Shack would love to hear.

As our visit was winding down and I got up to leave, Hughes came to the door to see me off and the last thing he said was, "When you get home, be sure and give my regards to the Hasler brothers and Harry in particular." The way the Game Warden was chuckling when he said that, it seemed like he and Harry were perhaps old friends from long ago, but it also rang strange that he never up and said so directly.

After pedalling the seven miles back home, my first call, of course, was up to The Shack as I was just bursting with all this news, especially the part about how there was now a fellow northerner living at Cloverdale who they could go and visit when they went there to provision up. But the reaction at The Shack was not entirely what I had thought it would be.

The part of my story about the problem of getting a trapping licence brought a nod of forgotten knowledge from Tom and Harry, and Tom apologized for forgetting that underage kids could not buy an unrestricted hunting licence.

"Do you think your Dad will sign for you?" he asked me.

"Oh sure he will," I answered, "because then I will be able to legally carry a gun when an adult is with me, which will mean I can keep a gun at our house so I can get rid of some of those deer that are chewing up our apple trees. I'll be able to plug those deer right off the back porch." This was really just speculation on my part, because the subject of whether Dad would sign had been creating a quandary in my mind all day. I did have the foresight to check with the Game Warden if it was okay if only one parent signed. He had assured me it was okay and furthermore, it didn't matter which one signed. So there was already a back-burner plan. If Dad refused the offer to sign, there was a good chance that Mom could be persuaded to do it as she was wise enough to dislike those deer more than Dad did. This did not completely solve the problem though, because Mom did not enjoy riding in cars, so she rarely went to Cloverdale. One time when it was considered almost necessary for her to go, she was offered a ride over with the Haslers in Almont's big new car, but she declined that offer by remarking she was not a good enough swimmer to get out of a submerged vehicle. Mom could be much too much of a nervous Nelly. As far as I knew, Almont had only ditched his car the once and it had shook him up enough that he had sworn on everything holy and liquid that it would never happen again. Mom still wouldn't buy it, so she sent me to do the shopping instead.

Tom had another dampener now as he reminded me, "You still won't be able to legally use or pack any of these guns because these are all rifles and pistols and it's not legal to use them anywhere in Surrey because some goddam fool passed a law that all hunting around here has to be done with a shotgun, and you ain't got one."

That was true and I already knew it, but for some time there had been another back-burner plan simmering and this seemed like a made-to-order time to move it up front, so I asked Tom,

"Tom, have you ever thought about buying a shotgun to shoot ducks and pheasants with? If we had one, we wouldn't have to keep it hidden in a sack when we walk down a road, and with slugs it will kill a deer almost as far away as the 32.20 will. You could even carry a legal shotgun in Almont's car to shoot ducks in the ditches on the trips over to Cloverdale. And I heard the Lewis brothers say that in the headlights of a car at night it's real easy to knock down a deer with a load of buckshot too."

For some reason, Tom could not see the logic to this and he and Harry laughed it off as Tom responded, "I've never had any use for a shotgun and I don't like these fish-eating ducks from around here. As for the pheasants, we got a kid that can clip their heads off with a .22 and that's a lot cheaper than using a shotgun."

Harry was sitting in his regular roost, laughing and rocking as usual, and he said to Tom, "You can't blame the kid for trying."

So it seemed like Tom, at least for the moment, was going to be difficult about this, so I changed the subject back to the visit with the Game Warden. I started out by saying, "Mr. Hughes thinks he met you guys up north somewhere."

Both Tom and Harry lowered their gin mugs, and Tom gave me that funny squinty-eyed look that he sometimes used and asked, "What did you say his name is?"

I repeated it and then he and Harry looked at each other as they shook their heads. Harry said, "I don't remember any Game Warden up there by the name of Hughes."

I clarified the situation by remembering what the Game Warden had said. "Maybe it was during the time when Mr. Hughes was a provincial policeman."

I had never seen Harry almost sober up as fast as he did then. He popped up out of his chair and stood there staring at me as he hoarsely asked, "WHEN HE WAS A WHAT?"

I was just about to repeat what I had said, but Harry gave me a downer sign with his hand and exclaimed, "Oh, for Christ sake! And you say this guy is the Game Warden here now?"

"Yup," was all I dared to reply.

He sank back down into his chair and drifted off into one of his philosophical religious moods as he kept repeating in a softer and softer voice, "Oh for Christ sake, oh for Christ sake..."

Tom was still sitting in his chair and he picked his mug back up and had a good swig as he said to his brother, "It's gettin' to be a smaller world, ain't it Harry?" Then they both began to laugh as they raised their mugs to each other and had another good go at the UDL.

Even though the clouds seemed to be lifting, I decided that it might be prudent to forego the Game Warden's final salute that I was to pass on to Harry.

After a few days I finally built up enough nerve to try the "licence signing" proposition on Dad. Surprisingly, he was reasonably agreeable. Of course he made me swear that I would not abuse the privilege by taking any of Tom's guns out when Tom wasn't coming with them, but I had been expecting to make that concession, so agreed to all the unnecessary rules. This conversation was the picture of co-operation, so I broached another subject before the euphoria wore off. I warned Dad that when we went to visit the Game Warden it would be best not to mention anything about my past trapping experiences.

At that request, Dad sort of smiled as he replied, "So you have trapped yourself, haven't you? Now you might understand more clearly the trouble you can make for yourself when you tell lies. It takes a very sharp mind to be able to live on lies and get away with them, and about the only people who are able to do it are politicians and lawyers. And you aren't either one."

It's hard to produce a valid argument against that kind of evidence and advice, and considering that he had not yet signed the licence, I decided not to even try, so I simply nodded silently in agreement.

In the end he did sign for my licence, and from then on I didn't have to dodge from brush patch to brush patch. It helped straighten my neck back out because I didn't have to look backwards so much. Dad warned me about things like that when he told me, "You can usually tell who the people are that walk the dark roads, because they tend to develop shifty eyes and nervous twitches."

Later on, when I tried that one on Tom, he quietly nodded and added, "Those are the kind of people who develop nervous trigger fingers too."

As time went on, Hugh Hughes and I became good friends. He and Dad hit it off well too, but as far as I know he never did stop in at The Shack to renew old acquaintances. All of this kept my life in a continuous balancing act because I was bouncing around between three different philosophies, all interesting enough that I did not want to have to make a choice of one or the other. I did try to avoid telling lies to any of them and adopted Tom's suggestion of, "Just learn to keep yer mouth shut, and for God's sake don't volunteer nothing." That's a logical theory for short-term conversations, but how do you develop or maintain a friendship around it? I tried it both ways, and because I was born with big feet and a mouth to match I often ended up in some much too quiet and embarrassing situations. And from the mixture of all the above, my own philosophy developed into "Don't ever give up, because some how and some way, THERE IS A WAY." Within reason of course.

In those years, the Game Department began a project to feed pheasants during snowbound winters. The idea was not new, as most of the Mud Bay and Elgin farmers had been doing it for years, but I was learning that governments tend to be slow to catch on to anything that works, especially if it's simple and inexpensive. This time, when the government decided to cede to common sense it came up with a system that was quite a bit better than the farmer method.

The farmers fed the pheasants by leaving the weed seed piles from their threshing machines and combines right out on the edges of the fields. When it snowed, the farmers would go back out there and kick the piles open so the pheasants could just help themselves. The pheasants loved it. Most of the Mud Bay farmers were also hunters, which was probably the reason they did this so enthusiastically. It didn't really cost them anything, but one of the other bird-feeding techniques they used most certainly did. Some farmers deliberately left wide uncut swaths along the edges of their grain fields. This method offered the pheasants and lots of other bird species not only feed, but also the standing grain plants that were stiff enough to keep the snow from laying them flat, so the birds could burrow right down under the snow and feed in a more natural way.

The hunting potato farmers did their share too, as they often left what we called "pig-feed" spuds (small and/or damaged potatoes) out in their low-lying fields. Some of them even went so far as to plug the drainage ditches so the water would flood back and make the rotten spuds attractive to the ducks. A flooded bean field was best of all.

Some of the farmers who were storing hay in big old double-doored barns out on the flats used another method to feed those pheasants. They would leave the barn doors partly open so the pheasants could go in and feed on the chaff that covered the floors. Many of the birds stayed in there and roosted on the rafters at night. This method worked best if there were doors on both sides of the barn and both were left open so the pheasants did not become overly nervous about being trapped inside. As the old saying goes, "Hunger will tame a lion," and enough of that snow, when it stayed long enough, made wild pheasants almost as tame as chickens. Once the pheasants learned to take advantage of this arrangement, they loved it. So did the farmers' barnyard cats. It was quite a sight to walk up to one of those barns and watch sometimes as many as a hundred pheasants go flying out the doors and open windows. To a stranger who was not expecting it, it must have been downright astounding.

When the government became involved, Hughes had access to many of the farmers' seed piles and he used to sack some of them up and haul the seed around in his car so he could scatter it in places where there were no benevolent farmers, or at least no hay or grain farms. Another of his innovations was to drop some of the feed off with the local trappers all over the Surrey and perhaps Langley area. I never did find out how many trappers there actually were around there, but for sure there were more than the fellow who had been trapping the Elgin area before me and myself. Inside the municipalities there were no registered traplines as Tom was used to up in the north country. Down south, the Game Department simply sold licences to all comers and then we had to get permission from the landowners to trap on their private property. The public land along the rivers and road ditches was wide open to anybody with a licence. This open system was not a good one. It created hard feelings and perhaps even more than that as trappers could (and some did) lay their own traps just ahead of their competitors'. But anyway, however many trappers Hughes had licensed in the area, he would drop some of this feed off with each of us so we could scatter it in remoter places than he could get to with his car. He also asked us to scatter the feed in places where poachers were not likely to find and take advantage of it. This was a job that I willingly volunteered to do.

When the Hasler boys found out I was doing this, they made a lot of snide remarks about how convenient it was of me to keep the meat supply fat and tame so it could be used all year round. They were joking of course, and I do not remember a single instance when any of them tried to snipe a pheasant off my feeding stations. Tom did warn me away from feeding them too close to The Shack. He said at some point the temptation might become too much to bear. I took him at his word and did most of my feeding in the lower fields and on other people's property. I do remember one Friday steak night when all four of us were seated at the table and I was telling the others something about all the pheasant lives I was saving for next summer's nesting, which in turn was going to result in so many more pheasants to shoot next fall. When I had wound down for a moment, Harry turned to his brothers and commented, "You know, that bastard is beginning to get to this kid."

During one of those bad snowy winters, it must have been 1948, I set up a feeding station right outside my bedroom window. All it amounted to was a trench dug in the snow to the ground, about three feet wide by fifty feet long. The idea of having it close to the house was so I could monitor the number of birds that were using it. They came early every morning and at last light in the evening, so I was able to sit in the comfort of my warm bed and watch them. Some days there were up to sixty pheasants feeding there at one time, making the wildest racket that you can imagine. The cocks were the noisiest and most aggressive as they were always fighting for positions along the trench, like it made a difference. Considering the number of birds that fed there that winter, I should have made the trench twice as long, but just the same, there was always something interesting going on out there.

One time I remember Mom's big orange tomcat, Tom Tidy, figured he was going to get an easy dinner and I watched him making a stalk on a flock of about twenty pheasants. The pheasants should have been able to see him coming, but if they did they were not responding properly, so the cat was able to get right up to within pouncing distance. Just as he was about to pounce, when his tail went stiff and straight, about six of the rooster pheasants lurched straight up into the air, perhaps eight to ten feet up, and then came straight down on top of poor old Tom Tidy. They hit him hard enough to roll him over and the noise of him screaming and them cackling was unbelievable. Those pheasants never let up until he streaked for shelter under the porch. When it was over, it looked like there was about an equal amount of fur and feathers floating around on top of the snow. I never saw that cat try for a pheasant again.

Another thing about that feeding station was it allowed me to observe exactly what feed the pheasants preferred. I carried that investigation to the point where I sorted out several pounds of seed mixture, seed by seed, then set the stuff out in separate piles on the ground and watched to see what the pheasants went for first. There would have been a seed mixture of several different plant species from those threshing piles. The pheasants certainly appreciated my efforts as they gobbled some of the piles immediately, some they picked over, and some they never ate at all, but it's hard to remember what useful thing was actually learned from it—other than if a person is going to sort weed seeds by hand and eye, he had better be prepared to go cross-eyed. With that being the case, the investigation was only continued for a short time and after that the pheasants had to revert back to sorting their own seeds. When I told Hughes about my experiments he always encouraged me to keep right on doing them and suggested I write down notes on my observations so he could pass the information on "higher up," as he referred to it. It was a nice feeling to a kid to be appreciated that way, and it sometimes made me wonder a bit about the Game Warden stories I had listened to from the opposite side of the municipality.

Dad didn't appreciate this experimental test plot beside the house as much as the Game Warden did, and he often complained about the racket those rooster pheasants made so early in the morning. His problem was that he was being woken up about an hour earlier than he wanted to be, and as he said, his interest began waning after listening to and watching his third cockfight. "By the time you have watched three cock pheasant fights, you have seen them all," he informed whoever wanted to listen. His reaction probably also stemmed from the fact that he was not a hunter, even though he certainly ate his full share of game meat that other people killed and gave to us. With those dozens of pheasants feeding under his window, he used to chide me with comments similar to those from The Shack, like why did he have to work so hard to feed a lazy family when there was so much meat going to waste right there in our own yard? He was only joking of course, and after all, he was my Dad so could be trusted.

Sometime just prior to that winter I had been allowed, at age twelve, to buy my first gun, a Stevens double-barrelled, 12-gauge shotgun. It was second hand but in good condition, and I was allowed to hang it on my bedroom wall, even though I was still not supposed to take it out of the house unless an adult could be persuaded to come along with it. The system was adhered to some of the time, like if company was around, but as Dad still had to work five and a half days a week to make a living for us, and as Mom never had the best eyes or ears in the country, there were some unspoken compromises. These were to everybody's satisfaction as the gun put more meat on our table than the golden rule ever would.

I was still having to spend time at school, which meant it became standard procedure on my part to lie in bed as long as possible each morning, hopefully long enough to miss the schoolbus. The most common way that Mom and Dad countered this plan was to come into the bedroom, jerk the covers off the bed, and toss them onto a chair on the opposite side of the room. As they turned to walk out, they would repeat that godawful phrase, "It's time to get up." But there came a particular morning when it turned out a bit different. When Dad opened the door and came in, I was awake all right but had my head buried down under the covers, not admitting that I was waiting for the usual prompt. For some reason he was slow to give it. I listened to him move around, trying to figure out what he might be up to, and then I heard him open the window. Immediately I thought to myself, "Aha! He thinks that he is going to freeze me out of here. Will I ever give him a lesson as to who can stand the cold the longest. At least until after bus time." But his footsteps were telling me that he was still in the room and he was not going back to his coffee cup. Strange. With the window open I could hear the pheasants out there making the grandest racket. It sounded like there might be as many as three good cockfights taking place at once. Almost enough noise to make a person sit up and appreciate what was going on.

Then I heard another noise and my heart almost stopped. The sound was the breech lock on my shotgun snapping shut.

Even before my breathing restarted I threw the blankets off, and just as I hollered NO, Dad let fly with both barrels. Out in the yard there was another explosion of noise as who knows how many pheasants all took off at the same time. It looked like a hundred or more. But there were eleven others, all hens, that were flopping around in the snow. I was numb and speechless, but Dad spun around and dropped the shotgun onto the bed as he excitedly said, "Come on, let's get out there and wring their necks and get them out of sight before someone comes to visit."

As we both stood there staring across the yard, I thought to myself, "Out of sight all right, but there just happens to be about ten thousand pheasant feathers floating around on top of the snow." Not to mention the blood that was splattered around.

It took a few minutes for me to get dressed and by that time Dad had gone out and killed and stuffed into a gunny sack all of the larger evidence. He tossed the sack into the woodshed and came back into the house to have breakfast. All during that breakfast he was in a jubilant mood as he kept jibing me with questions like, "How many pheasants have you been able to kill in *only* two shots?"

His comments were making dents all right, but I was not about to admit it, even though it did cross my mind to draw his comparisons out to include ducks, because down on the river I had been able to sluice (shoot sitting ducks) eight butterballs with a single shot. I was able to keep control, which meant keeping my trap shut, as I ate breakfast in silence. Mom never became involved in the discussion other than to head off a possible confrontation that she could sense was building up by asking, "Who is going to clean all those birds? Because I'm not." She had long since laid down a ground rule in our house, "Whoever kills them, cleans them." The same rule went for fishing too.

Up to that morning there had never been the slightest question about who the "whoever" was intended to mean, but this new situation allowed for the "indignant and righteous" to trade places with the other end of the spectrum. This time it was my turn to set the silence at the table and I indulged to the limit. I really was angry too. I'm still not sure if my anger was sparked by having my experiment messed up or if it was loss of trust in my Dad, or perhaps I was just jealous because Dad did it before I did it myself. But I never gave him the benefit of the doubt.

By the time breakfast was over, Dad was not taking my indignation too well. Just as I was heading out the door to go to the bus stop, he challenged, "If you think that all of a sudden you have become so goddam righteous over what we eat and when we do it, then tonight when the rest of us are having pheasant pie, you can salve everybody's conscience by having a couple of extra spuds instead."

I was surprised that he didn't offer to top it off with boiled onions over parsnips, but I still made no concession as I answered, "And just how do you intend to explain the yard full of feathers to the neighbours?" Then I finished him off with, "And not only that, but what happens if the Game Warden comes in delivering more pheasant feed?" (In those days, the penalty for doing what had just been done was $500 and/or six months, and the judges often laid down the maximum penalty.)

We had a long driveway that connected to the King George Highway, and as I reached the halfway point, I stopped and looked back towards the house. What did I see but Dad out in the yard, wading around in the snow with a paper shopping bag in his hand as he chased down those pheasant feathers. He did not see me, and as I stood there watching him for a few moments, the entire scene looked absolutely ridiculous and perhaps even pathetic. After spinning the sight through my mind for a few more moments, I walked back to the house, threw my books and lunch onto the table, changed into gumboots, found myself a bag, and went out into the yard to help him. We filled the trench in with snow and then dug a new one, and Dad even helped spread the feed into it. It's for sure that we never bagged all the feathers, but what was left could easily be explained away to cockfights. That night we had one of the best pheasant pies Mom had ever made. But it was not until a long time afterwards that that morning's work was ever mentioned again.

The following morning as I was preparing to head out to the bus stop again, I discovered, clipped by paper clip to my lunch bag, one of those required "notes to school" explaining why I was legally not there the day before. When I had been bothered with them in the past, Mom had always written them or I had paid twenty-five cents to a girl at school who was a handwriting genius, but this time the note was written and signed by my Dad.

Over the next few years, Hugh Hughes and I became pretty good friends even though I did play hide-and-seek games with him once in a while. Those diminished with time, but there were always those few grey areas, and perhaps down in Surrey there still are. For an example, there was one issue that the Game Warden, the Hasler brothers, Mud Bay farmers, and Dad all unspokenly agreed on, and that was the need to do a little quiet control work on the wild domestic cats and deer-chasing dogs. Tom let it be known that he did it all the time, but Hugh cautioned me once to keep such things to myself, and above all, not to ever mention such things to him. Only once did we ever break that code, when he asked me how I disposed of such things when they were caught in a trap or snare. Knowing that mentioning the existence of the "long barrel" might stretch our relationship further than common sense could allow, I replied, "Oh, I just slug them over the head with the back of my axe."

"Even something as big as a German shepherd?" he queried.

"Same thing," was the assurance.

The old Game Warden smiled with that twinkle in his eye as he finished the conversation, "I'll just bet you do."

So that's the way it was with the Game Warden and me, and I respected him for all of the different things he sparked into my mind. Later on, during the winter I left home, one of the last things I did was make my rounds of the farms and bid a few of my older friends good-bye, and Hugh was one of them. As I got up to leave, Hugh and I shook hands as he bid me farewell, and his last words were, "It's a great country and life you are heading for up in the Chilcotin. There is still space enough up there for a person like you to do pretty much as you please, and I wish you all the very best of luck while doing it. My only other advice is to go there and enjoy what you do, but for God's sake try and keep as far away from the temptations of trouble as you can. I'll be keeping an ear on you through our department network, and perhaps when you get settled in we can meet again." By this time he was sort of chuckling as he finished with, “If you can tie one up for me, I would love nothing better than to come up and go moose hunting with you.”

But again, it was one of those things that was not destined to happen.

Taken on the steps of Elgin school in 1946 or '47, this is the only school picture I have (I'm right of the teacher), and it even shows me with my shirt buttoned to the top. That's what a kid gets for standing next to the teacher, who was the only favourite I ever had. Of course she was blond, well built, very pretty, and had a personality that shows in this photo. It all helped to tame a wild young boy.

Mother, Avis Choate, near our Elgin house, 1948. Dad, Fred Choate, stands near the entrance of his souvenir store, 1060 King George Highway, 1948. It was named the "Blue Spruce Rancheree." Below, me with Rusty at the Elgin house, 1948.

Rusty, in front of our Elgin home, and beside him my first love, a double-barrelled Stevens 12-gauge shotgun, which I was allowed to buy when I was twelve years old.

My Pacific National Exhibition first-prize rabbit named Sheba, about 1949. Rusty really took to the boat built in 1948. We spent many hours on the Nicomekl River. From then on I never had to borrow Bill Hadden's boats anymore. When I left Elgin to come to Chilcotin, I gave the boat to a school friend, Donald Verpy.

Semiahmoo School taken about 1990. When I went there, there was no shrubbery, just rocks and gravel, which gave it a close resemblance to a concentration camp.

Murray and Mary Sanford at Semiahmoo School's 50-year reunion in 1990. Murray was a long-time principal there and one of our basketball coaches.

Me in 1975 and 1994.

CHAPTER 4

INDIANS

Quite a while ago, like in 1950 or 1951, when I would have been fifteen or just turned sixteen, there came a turning point in my life. By that time I considered myself a committed man of the woods and water, which in my mind made me a white Indian if there was such a thing. I hoped there was, because I wanted to be one and was even the first and, as it turned out, the only kid in the area to have my head shaved into an Iroquois hair cut, which earned me a trip to the school principal's office to give my reason for doing so.

It's hard to explain why I felt this affinity because even though there were true native Indians living as close as three miles away on the Semiahmoo Reserve, and at least two of them were in the same Semiahmoo High School that I attended, there had been no direct personal contact between myself and them. I don't know why that was, as I did know that some of them were still hunting and fishing, although I never did hear of them trapping anymore. There were more Indians living somewhere along the North Shore of Vancouver, up at Sechelt, and along the Fraser River, which was not far away. Mom and Dad knew some of those people as personal friends and a few of them dropped in to visit from time to time, but for some reason they and I never connected. My parents had met these people during Dad's "donkey puncher" logging days, when some of the Indians had been employed in the same trade, and I can remember Dad commenting that some of his friends had been the best boom men in the business.

On top of this local situation, we were taught by our history books that ancestors of these same Indians had been settled here for thousands of years before my ancestors built the railroad into British Columbia, not to mention before the fur brigade people who had been here for about a hundred years before the railroad. But what's a hundred or two hundred years compared to thousands? All of this added up to the fact that we were living on what had recently been Indian land. I do not remember anybody attempting to deny it. But there was another small and quiet question that we were discouraged from asking and that was, when did the Indians concede land ownership to the Europeans? As kids in the 1940s and 1950s, we simply assumed that it had been conceded. It must have been, or how and why were we here? Somewhere in our schoolbooks we read of how Long Island was bought and what the Europeans paid for it, but we were never told how many trinkets our forefathers had to pay for B.C. Strange.

It is possible we grew up assuming that all Indians had been defeated in war. After all, every movie and book about the western movement of white settlers leaned heavily towards portraying battles in which Indians died gloriously in defeat. Where and when the battles occurred, this is usually what happened. But there were no known battlegrounds in B.C., or none that we were told about, so how and why did the Indians give us this land? Hardly anybody ever asked and we were conveniently never told.

As I've come to learn in the fifty years since, the Indians were defeated and it was done by using the most insidious tools of war there are. We simply turned them inside out by out-politicking and out-religioning them. Politics is based mostly on deceit, and Christianity has been twisted into the religion of power and commerce. The actual weapon used is called the "seed of doubt." We planted it well and it worked, and for a great many it still works today as it is a contagious and deadly disease. Because they were not much different from the rest of us, the Indians succumbed.

Do you believe in fair play? If you think you do, then take a look at things from this perspective, and I would like to hear your answer afterward. In all of the kid games we were taught, there was always a winner and the losers were taught to respect that position. There was a phrase for that and it went something like

"Learn how to lose with dignity." One of the most sacred rules invented by Europeans before they crossed the big pond, which became pretty much an international "common law," was that losers must respect winners during the race to raise flags over new-found land. Whoever got there first could claim it as theirs by right of discovery. After that it could also get see-sawed around by right of conquest, but another of the early rules was that we declared war first, and after it was over, the winner accepted a parchment from the loser that acknowledged defeat and submission.

When our white forefathers arrived on the North American shore, they did not find a vacant land but one that was well populated with people. They planted and raised their flags anyway. Those same adventurers told the inhabitants of this land that they came in peace. To prove their sincerity they liberally sprinkled the locals with trinkets, crucifixes, and disease, but they never declared war, or at least not until a while later.

Something does not ring true here, because the planting of flags on a populated land without going through the formalities of declaring war is a contradiction. We never had nerve enough to try such a deceitful trick over in Europe, so why were the rules changed over here? Or were the rules still the same, but one side had learned how to fudge them a bit, like by cheating? If that was the case, then in what other game that you know of are cheaters allowed to keep the spoils after they are caught? Among European nations and most others as well, there are longstanding rules that refer to this situation as "being in possession of stolen property," and the culprits have always had to return the swag.

Of course we do know that as time went on, one side or the other did open hostilities on the other, and our side, under the "might is right" banner, conquered all of North America east of the Rockies, and the Yanks did it on the west side too. Most Indian tribes fought at least a little bit, but a few decided to accept our assurances of good treatment and they bent rather than fought. By recent international rules this might be viewed as "conceding to overwhelming intimidation." A more legal-sounding term would be "being forced to sign under duress," which by today's standards means that after things have calmed down to more rational levels, the agreements can be renegotiated. But as we all know, the

Indians and whites who signed those treaties did so with full dignity and respect for each other and especially for another fine-sounding legal phrase, "the rule of law." I'm sure it's so. Just read our history books and look at the pictures in them.

By the time the Europeans crossed the big rockpile on the Canadian side of the border, somebody had changed the rules again as we no longer dealt with tribal councils but simply overwhelmed them, even though just a few years earlier we signed an agreement with the Brits, who allowed us to have Canada without a revolution, saying we would continue the tribal treaty system as we swept on down to the Pacific. Oh sure we would. And we would do it without declaring war, too. And to prove our good intentions we sent the unarmed missionaries on ahead to convince the locals that the soldiers, police, railroaders, settlers, and whisky traders were all following along on a path of peace. Have you ever read the story of the Trojan Horse?

And now I hear there is a new set of rules for the games to come, but for safety's sake they are being written with split personalities, or perhaps a more understandable description would be "with a double set of books." But good, liberal-minded Canadians don't play games that way, do we? Of course not. That's why we send our soldiers masquerading as "peacekeepers" to as far a shore as we can, so they can make the new heathens adhere to our interpretation of that "rule of law" again. After all, we have no need of such enforcement here, so let's keep the ball well "over there." It looks like the new phrase for this is "The New World Order." Those words have been taken almost verbatim right straight out of the mouth of Adolf Hitler.

By now you must be wondering why I have wandered so far off course from a story about a kid growing up, but this was exactly the subject that sparked my political and social awakening. In 1950, just the word "Indian" held a romantic and mystical meaning for me. In my shadow mind it had echoes of wilderness, wild animals, and most of all, the freedom to roam. I was always hoping that someone in our family would be able to prove that some Indian blood ran in my veins, but even today it appears that I'm what some of the Indians jokingly refer to as a pure son-of-a-bitch. Down south there is another description, a "lily-whiter." We never did figure out where I inherited my love of wilderness from, as all of the rest of the family followed the road to mechanical technologies. Perhaps my greening is a long skip back to when Europe was as forested as it is here. It's hard to tell and it really doesn't matter anyway. But when the reality of the 1950 Indian situation in B.C. finally caught up to me, we did not start out on a particularly positive note.

My parents were politically minded, well informed, and what was known as free thinkers. All three kids in our family were encouraged to be the same. To know and understand the world and universe around us, we were encouraged to read books and newspapers and listen to the world news on the radio. No matter how hard up we were, we always found a dollar a month somewhere to pay for a subscription to the Vancouver *Sun* newspaper (as a teenager I delivered it myself). Some of the books in our house were written by authors with the names of Marx, Lenin, and Stalin. And in the picture frame that hung over the piano were pictures of Churchill and Roosevelt. No sign of truck or trade with Mackenzie King though. And my preference was always Grey Owl and Mark Twain. However, it was a front-page story in the Vancouver *Sun* that jerked me up to reality.

The story was about a group of Indians living somewhere near Vancouver who were drawing some kind of public assistance without having to work for it. I do not believe that it was called welfare then, but it must have been the same type of thing. And it would surely not have been in livable amounts. I cannot remember why I picked up on this story, unless it was from listening to my older friends talking about it. In that case I would have been listening to the farmers that I sometimes worked for. In those days the Elgin and Mud Bay farmers were noted for being very conservative, so the idea that anybody, anywhere, might be receiving some of their tax money without working for it would have been anathema to them, and my young ears seemed to have picked up on it. That led to my next action, which must have stemmed from the idea of doing my friends a favour. Because I had permission to hunt and trap over hundreds of acres of their land, a little mutual assistance seemed in order.

I wrote a public letter to the Vancouver *Sun* about those Indians receiving public handouts. It was not a complimentary letter towards the Indians, and by today's standards it was probably racist too, but another reality of those days was that everybody who was sure they were white enough *was* racist.

This letter seemed like a good idea when I thought about it and wrote it, but when I showed my masterpiece to Mom, the whole thing flew like a lead balloon. I can still see Mom's reaction as she read it standing up, because she collapsed into a chair beside the kitchen table. For the next several moments she sat there staring at the letter, even though it was not very long. She slowly began shaking her head as she handed it back to me, and she said in a quiet and close to trembling voice, "Oh God, son, please don't mail that letter. Perhaps Dad and I have never told you, but you would not be here if it were not for a family of Indians who live over in the area your letter is aimed at." Mom then nodded towards another chair, meaning for me to sit down, which I did. She then continued the story, which went pretty much like this.

"A long time ago, when Dad and I were first married, it must have been about 1920, we teamed up with your Uncle Al and Aunt Helen and took up a timber lease to handlog up Jervis Inlet. We then pooled all of our money and bought an Indian dugout canoe that the men rigged up with a small gas engine that in those days was called a "kicker," and we loaded everything we owned into it. We started up the inlet with the canoe dangerously overloaded, but everything was going okay until late afternoon, when we were a long way up the inlet and a tugboat passed us going the opposite way. Well, a few minutes later their bow wave caught up to us and over we went. By that time the tug was a half mile down the inlet and I guess nobody was looking backwards, as it just kept right on going. With the big load that was lashed into the canoe, it went straight to the bottom, so that left us swimming in circles on the surface. We could see the canoe a long way down there, but it was too deep to dive to and none of us were really strong swimmers. It was almost low tide and it was still running out, so we were being swept along with it, but it was not taking us to shore and the shore was too far to even consider trying for. We were soon swept up onto a large, low-lying rock, so we were all able to climb out onto it. Almost as soon as we stood up, we spotted our canoe floating upside down and already well past us as it headed out to sea. We could tell that all of our gear was gone from it. It must have somehow worked itself loose. But just the same, for any of our swimming ability the canoe was far out of our reach, so all we could do was watch it go.

"That rock was not very high out of the water, even at low tide, and we all knew that as soon as the tide turned to come back again we were going to be in deep trouble. There were not many boats or people travelling the inlet in those days, so we knew we were in a very bad situation unless a rare boat or at least some driftwood that we could use for a float to ride off on came by very soon. But by the time the tide did turn, not a damn thing had come within swimming distance and then the water began to rise. When you are caught that way, tides seem to rise faster than when you are on a beach, and in our case, when the water was over our knees, we knew we were doomed. None of us were very religious, but that evening I believe we were all trying to remember something about praying, because there was not so much as a straw in sight that was going to save us, and invisible prayer was all we had."

Mom began to smile a bit. She was obviously remembering those next moments as she continued her story. "When the water was almost up to our waists, we heard the put, put, put of a gas boat coming up the inlet, and sure enough, in a few minutes here came a family of Indians in a small fishing boat. Not only that, but they were towing our canoe! They spotted us okay and were able to come right up to the rock and then took us all to shore. They spoke pretty good English and told us that when they saw the upside-down canoe they figured somebody was in trouble, so they deliberately followed close to the shoreline to locate where the canoe might have come from, and that is how they found us. They gave us an old oar to steer with and a blanket to use as a sail and even enough food for a supper. The kicker was an inboard affair and still in the canoe, but it was full of water and useless. The Indians treated the entire situation as a great joke, and they kept chastising Rufe [Dad's nickname] and Al about trying to come up the inlet against the tide in such a small boat. The Indian man told our men. When you use these canoes, even with a gas engine, you gotta always travel with the tide. Even the Indians know that! When they told us that last piece, they seemed to think that was the biggest joke of all. And so that is how we were saved and were able to return to Vancouver the next day."

Mom and I sat there in silence for a while, staring at the letter until she pointed to it and continued, "I'm not going to try forbidding you to mail that letter, but I will beg you not to. I just wanted you to know that if it were not for that family of Indians, our family would not be here today."

She still was not finished with the story as she added, "All of that happened at a time when there were still white people around here who, if they saw an Indian family stranded that way, they would not have gone out of their way to help them as those Indians did for us. They did not do it for reward, because every penny we could beg, borrow, and steal was down there on the bottom of that inlet. The moment that canoe rolled over, we were all flat broke, and our family has never been able to make a restart since." Mom again nodded towards the letter as she continued, "As far as I know, that family still lives somewhere around the Vancouver area and it may very well be that your letter is aimed directly at them. Our grandparents' generation treated these local Indians very badly, and if we can make some small amends for them with such a small amount of money as the paper mentions here, then it will be only a smallest token of what we really owe them, and you should also take into account that most of those Indian people are a great deal poorer than we are."

By then Mom's story was beginning to slow down. As we both sat there still staring at my letter, the decision was made and I stood up, silently gathered up the letter and envelope, and took them over and relegated everything to the kitchen wood stove. Five-cent stamp and all.

After I returned to my chair, we sat in silence for a while until Mom got up and poured us both a cup of tea. Soon after, she began to speak again. "I know that you intend to leave home soon, and we know the direction that you will probably be going, so when you go, you must always realize that you are going to be living either with or very close to Indian people and on what, according to all types of laws, is still their land. Our ancestors never gave the Indians of B.C. so much as a single bead for this land, and neither have we, but someday there may have to be a settling of accounts over this. Don't ever try fooling yourself or anybody else, but the true facts are we live on stolen property and it's really just as simple as that. In some ways we are no better than Hitler was." (Mom did not think much of Hitler and she often told me that the most embarrassing day of her life was when I was born on his birthday, April 20, 1935, which was at a time when the last of the sane world realized what was loose amongst us.)

She had obviously not forgotten my letter yet, because she nodded towards the stove and continued, "Our people have done terrible things to our Indian neighbours, and there are some people who still do. I think it's become a camouflage way to cover up guilty consciences for what happened in the past. It's like trying to make the Indians and ourselves believe that it is somehow the Indians that are the thieves, and the system tends to deflect the criticism from where it really belongs. It works too, because most people are gullible enough to accept any theory that puts blame onto someone else's doorstep, and we can even be brought to believe that the lies we know are lies, are truth. There are people in this world who swear that they believe in God, Heaven, and the Golden Rule, and on Sunday morning they can be seen trying to buy their way through the Pearly Gates in hopes that God has not noticed what they have been doing all the previous week. I'm telling you these things in hope that it will give you warning as to what you and others can do to your mind. And don't you ever forget it," she added with emphasis. "Well, I've about wound down and I'm glad that you burned that letter, but there is just one other thing I would like you to consider. No matter how far north you end up going or what you do with most of your life, I do hope that you will never get into a predicament where you feel that you have to cheat or fight with the Indian people, because our ancestors did enough of that to last into eternity."

And with that she got up and went outside and left me with my own thoughts for a while. Mother must have had a powerful personality because even after fifty years that conversation and her presence are as clear as if we still sat beside her kitchen stove, watching that letter go up the chimney.

CHAPTER 5

POOL SHARKS AND GUTTERSNIPES

Almost every country kid eventually gets the urge to check out the seemingly interesting urban life. Our parents viewed it through different eyes. To them, urban life meant the temptations of city sin, which came in many varieties, and even back in 1950 we could pretty well take our choice. The parents didn't have it entirely right, though, because at that time White Rock was not a city and hardly even a big town. There were bigger businesses in Cloverdale, which still had the only liquor store in the area, and no town is ever going to become a city without a liquor store. Being the seat of the municipal government might have had something to do with Cloverdale keeping that business corralled to itself. But liquor wasn't the only vice the towns had to offer.

One of my older friends introduced me to another destructor of mind and time when he led me through the door of Bob Boucher's Pool Hall, conveniently located about half a mile away from the Semiahmoo School on the Johnson Road. That meant it was right beside the road I often walked home from school on. We lived exactly three miles from Semiahmoo, so I did have legal right to ride the schoolbus, but by the time I was fourteen I seldom remained at school all day as the last two work periods never seemed worth bothering with. Most Fridays were even shorter as it was a rare Friday that saw me at my desk after the lunch period. As any fool knows, it takes at least half a day to get primed up for a weekend. Mondays were not considered to be the best day in a week either, and even though I often got onto the Monday bus and arrived at school, by the time the first bell rang I could be so depressed by the sight of those walls that as the other kids drew books from their lockers, I would opt for my coat and slip out the side door into the real world. It was called "skipping classes" back then too, or if it was an all-day affair it was called "playing hooky." The Pool Hall had nothing to do with my missing school, as I was already addicted to freedom for other reasons.

As I remember, it was Jim Booth who first introduced me to the Pool Hall premises. A man (no women allowed) was supposed to be at least eighteen to pass through such doors, but by the time I was fourteen I was big enough that nobody ever challenged me. It was the same thing when I was seventeen and was supposed to be twenty-one to get into a beer parlour. There were a few advantages to growing up fast and being big.

Up to that time I had never seen the game of pool played. After sampling this urban indulgment off and on for a few months, I never became very impressed with it and was never as good a shot with a cue as I was with a shotgun, rifle, or pistol. I could hold my own at basketball and softball too, but my hand and eyes never meshed well over a pool table. Possibly the only reason I ever went back into a Pool Hall after the second or third time of choking through the cigarette smoke was because I was suspicious that those older boys and men were somehow having more fun inside those halls than I was on the outside in the fields and on the rivers. How else is a kid supposed to find out about things like that? Take somebody else's advice? Right.

Even though the game came across as being a bit nil, the stimulation from conversation in that place was something else, as home and school are not the only sacred halls of learning. There is a vast difference between being stimulated to learn by desire and being educated for need, especially when the need is dictated by "Them" and "They," which it usually is. As an example, back in the 1940s and early 1950s, where was a teenage kid going to learn the honest-to-God facts about human sex? Where did you learn about it? In a school classroom? Well I learned some there too, but it never compared to what we learned in a Pool Hall. In the school I went to there was a dull course called "Effects of Living," which could raise a person's interest a bit, but over at the Pool Hall there was an upgrade referred to as the "Facts of Life."

Us younger pool sharks always suspected that our new teachers were stretching a few of their facts, but now, remembering back to some of them, it is easier to accept that those stories were more fact than fiction. For instance, in later life I had the opportunity to compare those stories around the campfire with doctors, and they assured my side of the fire that there really were a few men who were endowed with twelve-inch pricks. One of those doctors was a psychiatrist and he added to the conversation by telling us there were women who preferred them. When the doctors realized they had an audience, they warmed up to the subject and told us eye-popping tales of nymphomaniacs as if they were warning us about something bad and dangerous. All the guys on our side of the fire were in their twenties then, and of course we thought the idea of a nympho being dangerous was a great joke, but then the psychiatrist asked us if we had any idea how many men actually died in the saddle. One of the other doctors backed him up and said he had attended the aftermath of a few of those situations, but he also admitted that they all died with a smile on their faces. Do you believe that a doctor would lie? Do you believe the men in the Pool Halls would lie? When those stories were laid on us as teenagers in the Pool Hall, they were warnings that bounced off like tennis balls because we considered ourselves pretty sharp and not as gullible as the teachers hoped. Now, after all the years of comparison, I wonder about some of the other things the sharks told us. One of those things got this sharkling into trouble that he didn't intend.

Teenage boys back in the 1940s were the smartest race of people that ever existed. If people wanted to dispute that statement, all they had to do was ask a teenage boy a question on any subject and he had the answer. At least he had *an* answer. Once in a while one of us had to ask questions, but only of very close friends or someone we trusted to confidentiality, because admission of ignorance could lead to self-destruction and that had to be avoided at all costs.

In my own case, I began running into new words that older people were using, especially around the Pool Halls. Since I didn't want to spoil someone's good story, I seldom stopped them to ask for word clarifications but just nodded in knowledge and laughed with the rest and thought a lot about it afterwards. You would be surprised at the different meanings that can arise from that type of self-education. There was one strange word being bandied about that I could not figure out the meaning of at all. I had even looked it up in the dictionary at home and the bigger ones at school, but the word was not listed anywhere and it had been bothering me for a while. Not all the words we heard or used were in those dictionaries, however, and we knew we had to be careful how and when we used four-letter words. I figured this one should be safer because it was a five-letter word, so one day I decided to get this problem settled out.

We all trust the advice of our fathers don't we? Dad and I were working on the woodpile, stacking it into the woodshed and discussing good, easygoing conversation topics, and it seemed an ideal time to broach the subject, which started out as, "Hey Pop, do you know what a dildo is?"

He had just picked up an armload of wood to stack onto the pile, but instead he slowly and quietly laid the sticks onto the chopping block. Then he stood up and stared at me across that block, a distance of about three feet, and I noticed his face had paled a bit, which was not a good sign. We stared silently at each other for a moment or two and he then brought up a roundhouse swat that hit me across the side of my head and almost knocked me down. It didn't hurt much, but it did stun me a bit, more mentally than physically.

As soon as I recovered my balance and was standing straight again, Dad stepped around the chopping block and stuck two stiff fingers against my chest as he stated in his quiet voice, "If you ever use words like that around here again, you are going to spend the next four weekends working on this woodpile, and that will be all day long too." He never did answer the question, and for the rest of that day we worked pretty much in silence.

We had another family confrontation over the value of a Pool Hall education, and it probably had an influence on how I made some of my later decisions. This time it was with Mother, as she had somehow gotten wind of where some of my school afternoons were being spent. She invited me into the kitchen to "lick out" the cookie mixing bowl. In our family this was considered to be a major treat. When the job was about half finished, Mom brought up the subject of the rumours she had been hearing about my presence in “those places.” Mom and I were good friends on other important subjects, and she had often supported my side of the argument when discussions came up about my midweek hunting and trapping forays. She was best at that when the forays were successful, when I would walk into the kitchen and lay on the table several plucked and cleaned pheasants, ducks, or grouse. Without even being asked she would write me out a couple of undated “letters to school” that explained why I had been legally absent from there the day before. The teachers still demanded those things right up to age sixteen.

This day Mom was not in such an expansive mood. She had other things on her mind which she brought to the forefront, and at the tone of her voice when she said the words “Pool Halls,” my alarm bells gave off warning signals. This Pool Hall thing had been going on for several months, and I had never thought that Mom would be interested in knowing about it so had neglected to inform her of my visits. After all, the money spent there was my own to spend as I saw fit, and it had always been that way. But it was not the wasting of money or the absence from school that was annoying her.

Considering that she was my friend, I decided to level with her as much as seemed necessary and reasonable. I admitted that the rumours she had heard were somewhat true and then gave her a much milder rendition of my experience with Pool Halls than she seemed to have heard. She let me tell my version without interruption, but I sensed from the way her mouth and chin were setting that it would be prudent to keep this subject as short and vague as possible, so I speeded up the cookie bowl job and shortened the story so I could fade out quickly.

This strategy was only partially successful, because when she saw I had about run my race, the lecture descended. Mom had been born in Iowa in 1904 and had spent only her first twelve years there before her family moved to somewhere around the Cypress Hills of Saskatchewan, but in the late 1940s she still used many Yankee sayings and expressions. By combining them with our West Coast Canadian, she had an expressive vocabulary. As she got warmed into this Pool Hall thing, she had me wondering if she had actually been inside one herself, as she seemed to know too much about them, including some things I didn't know myself yet. I remained as much ears and less mouth as possible in the hope that if I didn't dispute her opinions she would wind down faster. Perhaps this approach worked, but since I didn't know how long she intended to go on about this in the first place, I'll never know.

A couple of her warnings still ring in my ears as clear today as they did about 1950, and one of the points she hoarsely whispered was, "Do you want the neighbours to begin thinking of our family as being nothing but the lowest white trash?"

I had already been told the meaning of white trash, but just the way Mom said it that day made it sound like she figured I was about ready to bottom out in it. Just a few moments later she drove home another point as she asked me in the same tone, "Do you want to become known as a Guttersnipe?" Up to then I had never heard of a Guttersnipe, but remembering the ordeal with Dad over that other word, this time I played it safe and never asked for a clarification. Her tone and expression made it clear a Guttersnipe was not a kind of game bird she wanted laid onto her kitchen table, plucked and cleaned or not.

Mom's lecture may have had some effect on my abandoning the Pool Hall, but what really brought my visits to a slow close was my lack of interest in the game and especially the fact that I had to be locked in there with all that choking tobacco smoke. My Pool Hall education didn't last long, perhaps a year or so, and then I simply and gradually faded away from it. It was not all that different from skipping classes at the other school. Pool Halls and higher education are part of the urban life, and some of us are just not cut out for it. When a boy crosses the fourteen-year-old line, he soon learns that biology lessons can be learned almost anywhere and anytime two or more men get together. As a matter of fact, it's hard to avoid them. With that being the case, this kid gave up on the urban temptations and went back to the basic classroom of the fields, bush, and rivers. It was the place he knew he belonged.

CHAPTER 6

PICK AND SHOVEL MAN

It does not seem to matter how much money a kid makes, the damn stuff burns a hole in the pocket until it all runs out to who knows where. I was plagued with this problem just like the others. Trapping season was over at the end of February and my fur money was usually gone by the first of May, so that meant locating another source of income until the following December 1 when the season would start and life on the river would return again.

One of my year-round jobs was a paper route delivering the Vancouver *Sun*, which I kept up for about three years. In those days the *Sun* paid the rural carriers well, as the paper cost the subscriber a dollar per month and we were paid seventy-five cents of that, which meant either there was a huge profit margin in newspaper publishing or the company delivered to rural areas at a loss simply to keep up the prestige of publishing numbers. I think it was the latter. Rural paper carriers were hard to hire, as the distance between houses was often quite a ways, so our routes were long. Mine took about two hours on a bicycle and there were not a lot of customers, perhaps alternating between twenty and thirty.

The main reason I kept that paper route so long was that it gave me a chance to keep tabs on the game population and location throughout the year. It was also a good cover for packing a disassembled shotgun in my paper sack, because there were long quiet places along the Elgin roads where pheasants took deadly chances by allowing themselves to be seen. When I was fourteen I bought my first .22, a Model 60 Cooey repeater that could also be broken down to fit nicely into that sack. The drawback of the paper route was that it paid out only once a month. That's a long time for a young teenager, so there had to be instant income. In my case it came from pick and shovel work.

I cannot recall how I got into that business, but I do know that my reputation for being willing to dig spread the length of the Serpentine and Nicomekl flats, and any time I wanted such a job there was usually one to be had. When I think back on the reasons those jobs were available, I figure it may have been because it was a time in our social history when it was unpopular to be seen doing it. For instance, the school curriculum was promoting everything except manual labour. It was as if digging ditches, trapping, milking cows, planting seeds, and cleaning cow barns had become dirty words.

Another reason I got so many jobs might have been due to the difference between a good shovel man and a no-good one. The separation of the two had a lot to do with how many shovel handles they broke. In my own case, I have moved a lot of dirt in my lifetime but have broken few shovel handles while doing it. I didn't bring my own tools to the job very often, so when the farmer or other employer I was working for tallied up the job in the end, he was impressed by not having to replace shovel handles. Have you ever replaced a shovel handle? If not, then plan on a half day's job the first one you do because they do not go together easy, not if you want a factory-like result.

Shovel work turned out to be not anywhere near as dull and uninteresting as many people think it is. For instance, it's still a way better than working with intricate machines or computers because if you get angry with the job you can pick up the pick and beat hell out of the earth until you feel better. When you have relieved your temper, the hole is bigger too, so it's an all-plus affair. Just try the same system with a computer or vacuum cleaner. If more people would relieve their tempers this way more often, I'll bet this world would soon become a better place to live in. Furthermore, pick handles are durable and seldom break. So dig right in and you will feel a lot better for doing it. At least I did.

It wasn't just the soothing work of digging in the dirt that kept bringing me back to the shovel. It was also rewarding in the money angle. I dug my first septic tank hole when I was twelve years old, and the money for doing it built up so fast that in four days I owned a double-barrelled, 12-gauge Stevens shotgun that both my Dad and Tom Hasler said was in very good condition. The fellow in White Rock who sold it to me even tossed in an almost full box of Imperial number 5 shells for it. I used that gun for ten years and then resold it for thirty dollars again as it was still in good condition. Perhaps even now it hangs on some young hunter's bedroom wall as he goes to sleep at night staring at it, then dreams of the clouds of ducks as they come winging from Mud Bay into the spud fields behind the dikes on a winter evening. I hope so.

Another reason I took to those digging jobs was because Elgin farmers were reluctant to pay a teenage kid for work by the hour, so the jobs were done by contract, which meant there was no nosy boss checking on how and what I was doing all day. We simply pegged out the parameters of a hole, agreed on the price, and I seldom saw the boss again until the job was finished. That makes for a good and simple system of employer-labour relations, as things go better when the rules are simple. This was not always the case, though, because people are people and we tend to try levering advantages out of our neighbours, and that goes as much for labourers as it does employers. For instance, it did not take me long to learn that it is possible to deliberately inflate the value of a contract by convincing the employer that the ground is exceptionally hard, which means the job will take longer and require more money. Then if the ground turns out to be softer than expected, the digger pockets the difference. Of course the contractor can hook himself the other way too, as there are few people who have X-ray eyes that will detect the size and quantity of rocks that are hiding under three feet of soft topsoil. I found myself in both types of situations and they still stand out clearly in my mind.

The first time one of my contracts went sour was over a hole for a large gas tank and let me tell you, if ever there was a "sour gas" situation, this was it. At least for me it was. This particular contract was made with one of my best friends, Don Turnbull, who was fifteen or twenty years older than me. He in turn was the younger brother of Bob Turnbull, a long-time provincial policeman, game warden, and then Mountie at Alexis Creek in the Chilcotin. Don Turnbull had recently returned from doing his stint in the RCAF during World War Two and he had built a new Standard Oil service station and country store directly across the King George Highway from our place. This had rather mixed benefits for someone like me, as the temptations of store-bought stuff like candy and pop had just landed a mile closer than the Standish store at Sunnyside. The other side of the coin was that Don turned out to be a fellow hunter who owned several interesting guns. He was married by then and had two small sons who were way too young to be taken afield, so Don and I adopted each other. Tom Hasler was still there, but he was getting older by the year and seldom wanted to wander the fields and bush with me anymore, so he and I spent most of our time together sitting in The Shack trading stories. By 1947 or 1948 I had a few of my own to tell, and now that Don had arrived there was a whole new world of ideas and opinions to consider. Life was becoming more interesting by the month.

What I had to offer Turnbull was my knowledge of the area's bush trails and my positive contacts with most of the landowners, which meant we had expanded hunting territories. Don had a Dodge car, which allowed us to hunt in about a ten-mile radius of home for pennies' worth of gas (gas was twenty-three cents per imperial gallon). With Don being over eighteen, anytime we were together and saw a strange car coming, I did not have to hide my gun or take to the bush. He also began introducing me to the Sunday trapshoots that were held all over the district from Ladner to Burns Bog, Matt Kennedy's farm at Cloverdale, and up near Langley. The world was getting bigger. And being a large-sized country kid, I was able to fit into older company with hardly any problems. The majority of my friends were older and some were much older, mainly because most of the parents of kids close to my age would not allow their kids to have firearms (lack of trust, I guess), and since those instruments were my main interest, it tended to separate me from my same-age peer group. So Don Turnbull and I became best friends.

One day when Don was starting to do some expansion work on the gas station, he began digging a hole to drop a new gas tank into. In those days there was no such thing as a backhoe, and all other forms of power diggers were so huge that they were used only for road work and such jobs, so all holes smaller than a house were still being dug by hand. The year of this instance may have been 1948, and I know by that time I had expert advice to offer Don on how the hole should be dug. When I arrived at the site, Don was sweating away in the hole and had it down to about eighteen inches, so it was easy to see what the final result was going to look like. By then he had been working on it for two days and his explicit comments that came with every third swing of the pick indicated he was not enjoying the work like he should have been. So being his best friend, I began offering him every helpful idea that came to mind, like pointing out he did not have to swing the pick so hard as it was easier to take more time and scratch away with the point of the shovel. Then when he did have to use the pick, it would work much better if he took a few minutes each morning to sharpen it with his grinding wheel. It was all useful advice and coming from an expert too, and Don obviously appreciated it as he did try the slow-down-and-scratch-more idea, but he didn't get it quite right because the rate of dirt removal dropped off way below acceptable amounts. The bank he was digging into wasn't the easiest digging in the local area, but it didn't look like it was the worst either. What he was into was a firmly packed gravel streak that had some interesting yellow colour to it, so I asked Don if he had been taking gold pan samples as he was going down.

That was when his appreciation wore off, and the next swing of the pick saw it buried about four inches from my foot. He snarled at me in temper (he had one), "Look you big lazy bastard, if you don't have anything better to do than stand there yapping your mouth off, why don't you just hop right down here and show me how it should be done?"

Well he was right about a couple of points. With it not being hunting season, I had nothing in particular to do if I went home other than work on the woodpile, so I did willingly do as he suggested. Another reason for hopping in was that he had pricked my pride with the slur about being lazy. I knew that I wasn't, so it seemed like a good time to prove my ability. The truth was that there were no lazy country kids around Elgin as every one of us had our home jobs and our away-from-home jobs, usually on the larger farms, and we prided ourselves on our strength and ability. If anybody referred to one of us as a slacker, they were inviting a fat lip.

And just to prove that point to a doubter, when Don and I traded places the dirt really did begin to fly. The digging turned out to be about what it looked like it would be—"not the best but not the worst"—which meant it was not particularly hard to do, at least not for the Elgin badger. It must have been about 4 p.m. when I started digging in that hole, and by 6 o'clock, which was suppertime, the hole was six inches deeper all over. When Don came out of the store to advise me of the time, he was in a better mood and was impressed enough with my work to invite me in to have a cola. For free. (In those days pop came in six- to eight-ounce bottles that cost seven cents each.)

During the following conversation, Don did retract some of his earlier implications as he almost admitted that I might be a better pick and shovel man than he was. His wife Ilda was there and she chimed in and took that further as she suggested that I was probably the best in the country. Of course I knew that much myself and had already told them so. It was evening and Don got into one of his expansive moods and began telling me some of his wartime experiences, which used to turn me on. At some point he must have sensed the time was right and he changed the subject, inviting my expert opinion on how long it would take to finish that hole out there. It was to be ten feet long by six feet wide by seven feet deep, so the answer didn't take too much figuring. The hole was by then down to two feet, so it had five more to go. My estimate was that by working ten- or twelve-hour days, it should be done in two days, three at the most. There might possibly be some big rocks down there and they could be a problem, but adding the third day to the estimated two should take care of them. So I advised Don that he had better plan on three more days.

Don nodded in obvious agreement and then he tossed it to me. "So how much would you charge your hunting partner to finish digging it for him?"

Well now, my estimates had been thought out in terms of him digging his own hole, but this proffered job brought up mixed thoughts in my mind. The first was "big hole, big bucks," but the way he was smiling from behind the counter, I mellowed back down to the "best friend" reality. There was also the other reality the neighbourhood knew, which was that the Turnbulls were not rich like some of the farmers were, and I knew from travelling with Don that there were times he didn't have over five dollars in his pocket. There were no credit cards in 1948 either.

So how do you do business with a friend like that? In this case, time was not that important and with a weekend coming up, what the hell? As well, up to then I had never dug a hole that big, but it made sense to try something bigger with the aim of getting more experience and expanding my construction business and all that. Don was standing behind the counter and stacked up right behind him was the supply of ammunition that he had for sale. Part of that stack consisted of three unopened cartons of .22 cartridges. Two of them were Long Rifle size and the other contained .22 shorts. That meant there was a total of twenty smaller boxes of L.R. shells at fifty-two cents each and ten boxes of shorts at thirty-two cents each, and the total was exactly as you just figured because there was no sales tax. Well, again, what the hell? What are best friends for? I propositioned for his entire supply of .22 shells, which I thought was a better than fair deal for him.

Don didn't agree. He even acted like he might get angry again as he replied, "Jesus Christ, do you think I was born yesterday? If I let you have that many shells all at once, you will have every pheasant in the district killed off before any honest citizen has a chance at them." He had a way of exaggerating. At the same time, I wasn't sure if he was alluding to my marksmanship and hunting ability or the lack of pheasants in Surrey that year. Up to then, he and Stu MacBeth from Sullivan were the only people I was prepared to admit might be better with a .22 then I was. And this at a time in Surrey when a .22 could only be used on a licensed target range.

Don's statement gave me pause for a moment or so as I pondered another offer, but he beat me to the word. His counteroffer was, "I'll tell you what. If you finish that hole that is already damn near half dug, I'll give you the thousand Long Rifle shells and three colas a day while you are working in the hole. Not only that but I'll use the power grinder to keep your pick as sharp as you want it."

We stared at each other for a few more moments as I spun the thought, well, what are friends for if it's not to help each other in time of need? So I nodded in agreement as I said, "Okay, you got a deal."

Don smiled as he reached across the counter to shake hands and said, "A deal is a deal, and by God Ted, you are a good man. Almost."

I never did figure out what he meant by that last remark, but I did realize that we had just finalized what used to be known between friends as a "done deal." Don then turned towards that back shelf and I hoped he was going to hand me the .22 shells, but when he turned back towards me he had three malted milk chocolate bars that he handed across for free, too. At that time, pop and bars were all the same price. He must have read in my eyes what I was expecting, but he just grinned as he informed me, "When the hole is finished you get the shells, but not one until then." Sometimes that prude could sound like a schoolteacher.

So after school the next day I jumped back into the hole and started at it. As I remember, it was a Friday and I was able to shovel out another five or six inches of gravel before going home to supper. By this time Mom and Dad and most of the neighbourhood knew all about our "friendship" deal. I don't remember what the neighbours had to say about it, but Dad and my Grandad, who was living with us, were not impressed with my business ability and they kept harping that I had made a bad deal. I knew they were wrong, of course, and fully intended to prove them so. Dad, an old IWA organizer, said that this type of handwork should never be done by contract and I should have held out for an hourly wage.

My answer to that was "Yeah, but what if the boss doesn't ever offer the job for wages?"

"Then go look for a better one," Dad advised me. I had already learned there was no sense in discussing the matter further by pointing out there is a time when there are no other jobs, because his response to that was, "Just sit down and wait the bosses out."

And for how long do you sit and do nothing? Right.

Grandad, who was a retired banker, was pretty much on my side and his view of this latest contract was that I had simply given in too soon. He did agree that now the deal had been made, I had to carry it through as agreed. He did give me advice for the future. "The idea of being a businessman is to make as much profit as possible on a deal and let the other guy look out for himself."

Neither one of them would discuss the friendship side of deals, so I learned there are at least three sides to consider when making deals. But this one was done and it was time to get it behind me, though their contrasting opinions did make for interesting contemplation for the duration of my time down in that gas hole.

The job became serious on Saturday morning when I began a "set to" that made the dirt fly. I can now offer expert advice to anyone who might consider following that lead, and the first piece is don't ever take on such a job on a Saturday morning beside a public road in your own community where every lout and lass knows who you are. By the time noon came around I was becoming suspicious that some of my friends and acquaintances were making deliberate and unnecessary trips to the store just to check out the progress down where I was. And every goddam one of them had advice too. Hardly any of their advice had anything to do with the actual digging, as none of them were pick and shovel experts, but many of them considered themselves better business dealers. The first question they all asked was how much Turnbull was paying for this job. You would be astounded at how many different tones of laughter there are. By noon I had given up trying to explain the friendship side of deal making, as it was easy to see that nobody else around Elgin could see any merit to the idea. Perhaps the recent war had callused their minds. That's what Don suggested. It didn't matter anyway, because I had the thickest skin of any of them. Their comments may have even had a positive effect, because rather than jump up out of the hole and discuss the implications at closer range, I added it to more effort on the pick and shovel handles.

When some of the older farmers came to watch, they offered interesting advice and offers. One fellow, I think it was Old Bill Dinsmore, nodded in agreement at what I was doing as he commented, "It's about time the cost of that kind of work came back down to a sensible level."

Then there was another, name of Lloyd Cousins, who when his turn came said that when this job was over and I wanted another in the same price range, he had about a mile of ditches to dig. He was a friend too, but not as close a one as Turnbull was, so I took Dad's advice and opted out until the money offer went up. It didn't.

There were all kinds of digging jobs that needed doing, and in some cases the money offer was higher, even much higher. My reputation was being built. One farmer said if I would dig a ditch for him, he would not only give me the full 1500 .22 shells, but he would also throw in his own grandfather's old single shot .22 that still shot straight. And for friendship's sake I could have a box and a half of black powder shotgun shells that came from the same source. I told him that I would keep his offer in mind, because I knew that such a .22 had considerable teenage market value.

Another offer that was worth considering came from a farmer who was admiring my work and said if I would dig a ditch for him, he would up the offer to 2000 shells, a case of beer a day, and twenty dollars cash when the job was done. Now that man understood the real workings of the world. Although at thirteen I wasn't into the booze thing yet, I did know that my older teenage friends were used to paying a bootlegger anywhere from five dollars to fifteen dollars per case for beer that cost two dollars and ten cents at the liquor store. When I mentioned that offer to Don and wanted an explanation as to why one bootlegger sold beer for five dollars and the other was asking fifteen, he laughingly told me it had a lot to do with how many six-month stretches a bootlegger had to his credit. This was at a time when judges had a reputation for handing down doubled sentences for repeat offenders. "If you ever get into the bootlegging racket, the key to making money out of it is to never get caught the first time," Don warned us kids. And so the offers kept piling up.

After lunch on that Saturday afternoon, an eyeball survey said the job was going pretty well as estimated and by 2 p.m. I was down below the three-foot level, so knocked off for one of my free colas. Things were still going well as there was no sign of big rocks, so it was simply pick, pick, pick and shovel, shovel, shovel and the hole was getting noticeably deeper by the hour. Slow but steady, which makes for satisfying work.

It must have been about 3 p.m., as I was picking another layer loose, when one of the pick swings did not seem to chip up its intended bite. In fact, it felt like it tried to bounce back, but not like it had hit a rock. A few more heavy pick swings into the same area all brought the same feel and results, so laying the pick aside, I went to work with the shovel and cleared the loose gravel out of the hole so I could see what the problem was. After the shovel work, I dropped down on my knees to give a better cleaning job. It exposed a dull-coloured streak of soil that drove my heart right down into my lower innards. The colour definitely was not the glint of gold. I can still remember kneeling there, staring at that little patch of ground until the reality was firmly in place. Do you know what "blue hardpan" looks like and is? Oh God, and there was still about three feet to go. How unlucky could I get?

Blue hardpan was well known in that area and probably still is today. It had always been a favourite conversation point when wells or large holes were being dug by hand, but up until that day I had never seen it above about ten feet or so. Have you ever noticed how long it sometimes takes negative reality to become a mental fact? It's that way with me too, and it wasn't until I had picked all the gravel out of the entire hole that I accepted there was a full carpet of hardpan down there. Well I couldn't give up, and there was always the possibility that this was just a shallow layer and the next pick swing would sink right through into something like soft beach sand. It could happen, but this time it didn't. The job had just dropped into bull-low gear.

Jim Booth, who was Don's assistant mechanic, thought the situation was just oh so funny, and he spent the rest of the day cackling remarks that were becoming as old and unwanted as a spawned-out salmon. He tried making up a song or rhyme to fit the line "a deal is a deal" into. The rest of the lyrics from his warped thinking were no better either.

Turnbull was a bit more sympathetic and kept trying to reassure me that he never knew the hardpan was so close to the surface, but as I sat on the edge of the hole contemplating my next plan of action, my mind was becoming tainted by skepticism. When you were thirteen, did you understand the meaning of reneging on a deal? I didn't either, and there were no teachers at hand. Then there was pride, which should be taught as being only for other people because it is one of the "top ten" elements of self-destruction. And how were you at renegotiation when you were that age? My Dad was known as a provincial authority on it at that time, but I didn't realize it so never went home to ask for his opinion. Instead, with Booth's song ringing in my ears and under Turnbull's wondering stare, it was back down to the bottom I went, without the enthusiasm of that morning.

Have you ever dug into blue hardpan with a pick, bar, and shovel? If not, then I'll enlighten you right now. Don had a heavy bar and a pick to match, and he did keep his word about keeping them razor sharp for me, but a full overhand swing with either chipped up a single wafer of blue clay that was maybe a third of an inch thick and the size of the top of a Pacific Milk can. And I still needed to dig another ten feet by six feet by three feet. Today, with a ten-dollar calculator, which at that time did not yet exist, a person could figure out how many swings with the pick it was going to take to finish the job, then figure the shovelling and maybe go back and add another few thousand pick swings for the times you hit a rock and chipped up nothing. In case you have not yet figured it out, the hole did not get finished that weekend. It took every evening of the following week until dark and two full hooky days before the next Saturday, when Turnbull gave his nod of approval.

On top of the hand-blistering work that week, I also had to put up with nightly family advice that was like a broken record. Every supper brought forth Dad's financial estimates of what I would have been making if the hole had been dug for "honest hourly wages." My reply to that was I didn't think Don had that kind of money to sink into the hole. Anyway, it was just like all the neighbours kept telling me, "A deal is a deal," especially among friends. "Do you expect me to cut out on my best friend?" I asked him. To that he would just stare out the window as he shook his head.

Grandad didn't budge much on his updates either, as the old banker's final advice on the subject was, "To succeed in this world you have to learn to grab as much as you can from wherever you can and let all the others look out for themselves. And don't you ever allow yourself to be conned into believing there is such a thing as a friendly dollar." Perhaps they were right, but I used to lie in bed at night thinking about it and hoping they were wrong.

The day that Don and I settled up our accounts over the gas hole, we were back in the store with him standing behind the counter and me sitting on a stack of wooden pop cases across from him. He reached to the shelf where the ammo was stored and picked up the two cartons of .22 Long Rifle shells and laid them out on the counter as he said, "Well, there you are. And I sure as hell hope you don't use them to kill every pheasant between here and Langley before the season opens."

After he and Booth and I finished laughing that one off, I casually suggested that because the hole had taken so much longer to dig, he ought to relent and add the carton of .22 shorts that were still on the shelf behind him.

To my appeal, Don stood a little straighter and took on an indignant expression as he laid it back onto me, "Are you kidding? Do you realize how much your slow digging has cost me? That hole was supposed to have been finished by last Sunday and we should have been pumping gas out of it by Wednesday, but now with the weekend here again I can't make a cent out of that deal until this coming Wednesday. And not only that, but when I offered you three colas a day we were figuring it on a three-day deal at the most, but you dragged that job into eight days, which cost me over a case of cola. You or your Dad should be offering to pay me for at least half of that case," he ended emphatically.

How does a teenager argue with that kind of rationalizing? Personally, I decided the easiest way was to drop the subject, take my shells and experience, and go home, which I did. Don never did try billing Dad or me for those extra cola either.

It wasn't quite over, because that night I had to take the last blast from Dad and Grandad again. We sat down to a leg of store-bought mutton that Dad hated the sight, smell, and taste of as it reminded him of the trenches of World War One where he had eaten more than a lifetime's fill of it. I had stacked my .22 supply in plain sight on the shelf of the buffet and spent most of the supper period staring at it, and Dad must have noted this and read my mind because he commented, "Well I hope you learned something from that deal. If you go taking contract deals again, you had better learn how to test a job out before you bid on it and don't be afraid to bid high, because you can always lower your price but it's impossible to raise it. And that sweetheart deal you offered your friend was about as stupid as offering to volunteer for some job in the army."

Grandad had it figured almost the same way. He had been sitting there chewing on his pipe, listening to us, and he began to chuckle as he advised me, "In Don Turnbull you have a good business teacher, so you pay attention to how he operates because I have a hunch that if he lives long enough, he will die a millionaire."

After a week's hard work and all the proffered advice, my mind and body had become numb to both and I guess Dad sensed it. He finally relented as he nodded towards the stack on the buffet and said, "Why don't you take a few of those down to the lower fields and see if you can get us something better to eat than this damn poison that your mother is trying to kill us off with?"

The blisters wore off and the neighbours found another scandal that was none of their business but took the heat off of me, and I took on another digging contract that had different but not so different end results. This time there was no thought of offering a "sweetheart deal" as Dad still referred to the gas hole affair. This was a well-thought-out contract. Just as I had been advised, this time it was soil tested, plotted out, and counted out and it could not possibly go wrong. Furthermore, the deal was with a fellow farmer. How many more assurances do you need? But even now, after fifty or so years, I can still sometimes taste the bitterness of that deal.

This time the contract was for digging post holes. The way it started was, this farmer had recently hired an older pick and shovel expert to dig a line of holes for an hourly rate of seventy-five cents per hour. Apparently something in their agreement went wrong and the farmer figured the holes were not being dug fast enough for the money he was paying out, so he fired the digger and made contact with me (he was one of the farmers who had kept tabs on my gas hole contract enterprise). To simplify things here, let's just refer to this farmer as "Con." I forget how he sent word to me, but however it was it sounded interesting enough to go and visit him at his farm. He told me the story and we both walked out to the proposed fence line, where the line was already pegged out. For the time he had been there, the former shovel man had dug very few holes and Con had it figured out that they cost him $2.50 each, which he also figured was more than they were worth. Con made several references to the former digger as "that goddam Union Hall son-of-a-bitch." I never bothered mentioning to Con that my Dad was a union organizer, as it didn't seem like he would be interested. We agreed that these holes were overpriced, and when I examined the soil consistency, the number of dug holes compared to the amount of time digging did not make sense. These holes were thirty inches deep in soft black dirt that could be dug with very little bar work and no picking.

After we discussed the job in a vague way and the weather in more detail, Con asked me how much I would charge per hole. He said there were exactly 200 more that were all pegged out. Remembering all the recent conversations at home about not underpricing contract work, and considering that Con was not the type of friend Turnbull was, it seemed like he was fair game so I made an offer of $1.25 per hole.

Con thought for a moment and then shook his head as he told me, "It's still too much because I know that those holes can be dug out a lot faster than that Union Hall son-of-a-bitch was doing them."

So we dickered for a while and we ended up with a mutual agreement of 200 holes at one dollar per, all to be paid out when the entire job was completed. This must have been in 1948 or 1949, when a dollar still bought something, so this job was going into the real big money league, even paying more than trapping—providing we were right about that soil consistency. The timing was right in other ways too, because it was early fall, just before hunting season, and that shotgun I had was turning into an expensive partner to feed, so this amount of money was going to come like manna from above.

The day was still young as it was midmorning of a Friday on which, for some reason, I had not bothered to go to school, so it was as good a time as any to get started on this new job. We measured out a thirty-inch mark on the shovel handle and Con, just before he went back to his house, said, "Well now you can get right at it," so that's exactly what I did.

This time things didn't go as planned or hoped; they went better. If Con figured the digging should be easy, he didn't realize just how easy it was and I could hardly believe it myself. After the first few holes, time flew by and I was able to slip my mind into one of those mellow but conscious situations where work becomes something else. In this case, going across that field with thirty-foot pauses to dig those holes, all my mind was doing was adding dollar, dollar, dollar. When you have only a nickel in your pocket and it's your only nickel, thoughts like those can become as intoxicating as your first bout with a full whisky bottle.

By the time the schoolbus passed by around 4 o'clock, there were fifty-five holes dug down to over thirty-two inches each, so I hid the shovel, grabbed my coat, and headed for home as if I had just stepped off that bus. When it seemed practical to coordinate things like that, I often did, as Mom and Dad would get into spells when they would lecture me about missing too much school. I tried to soften the realities for them as much as possible. It's hard to say how often they believed I had gone to school, but timing my appearance with the bus give them a mental "out" to avoid dealing with behaviour they couldn't control anyway, and it gave me the experience of practising a "wide-eyed country boy" innocence on the older generation, so we all benefited.

I wasn't going to go straight home though, as I seldom did even if I went to school. My usual first stop was Turnbull's garage, which had become the afternoon gathering spot for most of the men and boys in the local area. It seemed wise to avoid having any more to do with Con before the job was finished—then he could be surprised with the whole thing all at once. When I arrived at Turnbull's, most of the regulars were already there so I gave them my full rendition of the newest contract. Even some of the other farmers admitted it was a good deal for both of us, and Don Turnbull said he figured he was entitled to something he referred to as a "finder's fee" for giving me the exposure and experience in his gas hole. He said it with a laugh, though with him you just never knew for sure.

Bill Bjorneson, one of my older hunting buddies, was there and when he heard what my take from this post hole job was going to be, he said he knew where a person could buy a "like new" Model 1897 Winchester shotgun for seventy dollars. Or if I was interested in a real upgrade, a brand new Model 12 Winchester shotgun for a hundred and ten dollars. That was the type that Don used. It was a damn good gun and his shooting with it was right up in the tops, too. The doors that open to the sounds of money! More job offers, guns, and adult respect. In that kind of company, teenage peer respect doesn't even rate thought or mention.

During supper that evening I casually mentioned to Mom and Dad that I had stopped by Con's farm that afternoon and had taken on a digging contract. Before Dad could get launched into another of his "get a better deal" lectures, I told them in one sentence what the soil was like and what the loot was going to amount to. This time Dad nodded in agreement and admitted that it sounded like a situation where "honest labour and honest pay" would mesh together. There were times he seemed to overuse that phrase, and it reminded me of a song I heard a bunch of the IWA men singing in the Union Hall in New Westminster with lyrics that went, "We want eight dollars a day for eight hours of work." Those big men really belted out that song, standing there waving their arms and fists about. When I mentioned the song to Turnbull one time, he said it sounded to him like they were a bunch of Communists and he didn't seem to have much use for them. I was willing to bet that Con and the rest of the Mud Bay farmers would not be much interested in hearing it either, so I accommodated and put it out of my mind for a long time.

Dad's other comment about my new job was that he was willing to bet that I could do the job in the following two weekends. It did not seem necessary to reveal to him that the job was already one quarter done or what I intended to do with the fortune when I got it, so we spun the conversation in another direction, which I believe was about an upcoming school basketball game. What was really on my mind was the fact that with the present weekend to work on it, followed by a Monday that was seldom worth going to school for, I could have that job finished by mid-Monday, get my money, and have one of those shotguns by Wednesday. There were also thoughts of buying both guns and still having enough money to buy several boxes of shells and a new pair of basketball shoes that I needed. After all, there was no sense leaving money lying around while prices got inflated, and this was beginning to happen, though the word was not yet in general use.

Shortly after sunrise on Saturday morning the digger was already into a full sweat, and by midday I knew that this contract was everything the gas hole wasn't. By the time darkness fell, I was exactly 150 holes across the field, which meant there were only 50 more to go. Incredible! From there I knew that it was all black soil to the river and nothing could possibly go wrong. The job, the guns, and everything were in the pot.

Darkness or not, no red-blooded kid goes straight home without telling the world and sundry what a great place it is, so I stopped off at Turnbull's store to enlighten them. When Don heard the number of already-dug holes I was laying claim to, he gave me a curious look and suggested that I had better go back over them and make sure they were ALL down to below thirty inches. I was way ahead of him, as every one was thirty-two-plus inches and a few, by accident, were more like thirty-six inches. That's how easy the digging was.

When I arrived home and told Mom and Dad how things were going, Dad also got one of those quizzical looks on his face as he asked me, "How in the world could you possibly have dug 150 holes in one day?"

"I dunno," I answered. "I guess it's just that I'm the best badger around here."

Then he too went through all that baloney about making sure there was actually a little more than thirty inches to the depths of the holes. I was able to assure him I'd already done as he suggested and was hoping that he might volunteer to come down next day and check my claims out, as the walk would teach him a lesson for even considering to doubt my word. But he didn't.

It wasn't to church I went at daylight on Sunday, but rather back to the gold field and by 2 o'clock the job was finished. The last hole was in the Nicomekl dike, where the larger end post was to be set, so on my own initiative I made that hole wider and down to forty inches. It was DONE! Talk about luck. Out of 200 holes, the shovel had never touched a rock or a stump.

As I sat there on the dike and stared back down over my work, it gave me such warm thoughts that there was even room to consider the possibility of going to school on Monday after all. I picked up the shovel and walked back towards Con's house, where I knew he was working. There was still lots of daylight left if he wanted to check my work out before paying me. I can still remember wondering, as I walked down the fence line, whether he would pay me in cash or by cheque. It would be nicer if it were in cash, like perhaps in twenty-dollar bills. I had handled few of those in my life. Maybe only a couple. Those bills were just barely common, as most money transactions were still being done in twos, fives, and tens. There were still lots of silver dollars being used too. And when was the last time you saw a four-bit piece (a fifty-cent coin)? At that time we still got change back from a four-bit piece when buying two imperial gallons of gas. I had not yet even seen a fifty- or hundred-dollar bill. I loved the feel of money.

When I arrived back at the yard, I located Con at work under his homemade tractor. He heard me walk up and stuck his head out from under as he smiled and said, "Hi, how are you making out down there?"

"All finished," I answered.

He didn't reply for a moment, but when he did he stuck his head out a little further as he gave me a quizzical look and inquired, "Oh yeah? What did you do, get a bunch of other kids to help you?"

"Nope, did it all myself," was the truthful reply.

His gaze became more quizzical as he asked me with a bit of a bite to his tone, "Oh, come on now. Are you trying to tell me that you dug 200 holes, thirty inches deep, in that amount of time?"

"Yup," I replied, "and every one of those holes is over thirty-two inches deep and some a lot deeper."

About then the quiz went off his face and he hoisted himself out from under the tractor. When he stood up, he didn't say anything for a moment but stared back down at his field. He turned back to face me as he said in a quiet voice, "Have you got any objection if we both go down there and check those holes out?"

I had no objection at all and was fully expecting that we would be doing exactly that and had even left the shovel with the marker on it standing in the first hole. I mentioned all of this to Con. He nodded towards the field as he started moving out and said, "Okay, let's go look it over," but by this time I noted a cooler and harder edge to his voice and I could not understand why.

Con and I were about the same size, so it didn't take us long to hike down to the beginning of the new fence line. He brusquely grabbed the shovel, checked the depth of the first hole, and as we walked towards the next hole it looked like he was eyeing the marker on the shovel, perhaps checking to see if it had been moved. It hadn't been, and the idea of doing so had never even crossed my mind. By the time we arrived at the second hole he was obviously comfortable with the marker position and he stuck the shovel down and nodded in agreement, the same at number three and so on down the line. It was somewhere about the twentieth hole when he turned to me and said, "These holes must have been pretty easy to dig."

My reply to that was, "Yup, they sure were."

Con gave me a strange-looking stare that made my mind flutter for a moment or two as a new thought spun through, warning me that perhaps I should not have been so candid. Because I had to explain every little thing to teachers all the time, I had concluded that it's not always in a person's best interest to tell the entire truth about some things unless there is no other way out. It seemed a person could make more mileage by dribbling the truth out and being ready to stop as soon as the listener appeared satisfied. Now I had the feeling my mouth had just dribbled too much, but whatever damage may have been done was done. The damage control system kicked in as we walked to the next hole where I casually commented to Con, "I think your hired man cheated on his job a bit."

He didn't reply right away, but as he was pulling the shovel out of that hole he stared straight at me and exclaimed in a frosty tone, "The next time I meet that bastard, I'm going to spike his nuts to a stump." I got the impression that he meant it, and it created a strange tingling sensation somewhere down in my lower belly.

When we arrived at the last hole, Con stopped and leaned on the shovel for a few moments as he stared back up the fence line. It was plain to see that he was thinking but not about to speak. I felt uncomfortable so I broke the silence by asking, "Well, are the holes all okay?"

His only reply was a slight nod that appeared to be of agreement and he then shouldered the shovel and we both started the hike back towards the buildings. Con was obviously angry, but I could not imagine how it might be directed towards me. I was feeling thankful that I wasn't in that Union Hall son-of-a-bitch's pants, because there were always stories floating around the country that suggested some farmers became a bit strange in their old age. The general feeling I had was that I should be cautious. The silent walk back was tense enough that all I wanted was to get my money and get away from there, and I was feeling relieved that Con and I had shook in full agreement for a "deal is a deal" contract.

When we arrived at the back door of the house, Con threw the shovel up against the wall and turned to stare at me, still in silence. It made for a squirmy feeling so I broke the impasse by saying, "Well, if the job is all done, then I might just as well head for home." I never mentioned anything about payment but was hoping my voice implied it so he would do it voluntarily. It worked because he drew out his wallet and then flipped out two twenties and a ten to me and sort of forced them into my hand. I could see that there was still a large sheaf of bills in the wallet, but he quickly flapped it shut and replaced it in his hip pocket. He did not say a word and neither did I. I just stood there with the fifty dollars in my hand as I stared at him.

This time Con broke the silence to inform me, "That's all that goddam job was worth. If you think I'm paying a schoolboy your age two hundred dollars for two days of work, then you better think again. Even at fifty dollars you are still being very well paid for that type of work," he emphasized.

I was dumbfounded and began to tremble as I asked him in reply, "But what about the deal of a contract?"

"To hell with contracts," he almost shouted at me. "Nobody pays a kid your age that kind of money. Do you think that I'm going to let myself become the laughingstock of the country?"

By this time there were hot and cold thoughts racing through my mind, and one of them was to size Con up a bit. He and I were about the same in height, but he was heavier and a very strong-looking fifty-year-old, so that thought died about as fast as it came up. And anyway, in the 1940s no thirteen-year-old kid was allowed to stand up to an adult that way and in hardly any other ways either. Teenagers still had, and most knew, their place in society and in no way was it equal to an adult's. In many cases our position was much closer to zero.

There were many different jokes and old folks' stories about the price of experience, and a person often wonders if and when the payments ever cease. Thoughts like that spun through my mind that day too, and after standing there on the step and staring at each other, I was the one who blinked by silently putting the money in my shirt pocket, then turning and walking away. As I walked across the yard, thoughts of revenge lay heavily on my mind and there were tindery looking buildings standing there, but luckily for both of us, perhaps, it never ended that way.

While heading towards home with slow and heavy steps that afternoon, I made the regular detour over to Turnbull's store and related my problem to my best friend. All he said was, "Oh for Christ sake. Well, tell your Dad about it, and if Con doesn't settle up with you soon, I'll mention it to him when he comes into the store and maybe we can embarrass him enough that he will settle with you."

After pondering Don's advice for a few moments I was still mighty suspicious about how it was all going to turn out, so I asked Don, if he saw Bill Bjorneson before I did, to tentatively cancel the shotgun deal. Don nodded quietly.

Then it was time to cross over to home and confess my latest business shortcomings. When they heard it, Mom just listened as she stared out the kitchen window, slowly shaking her head in silence. But Dad surprised me as he got very angry in his quiet way and quizzed me in all directions about the deal. When he was satisfied, he grabbed his coat and headed out the back door as he said to me, "You stay right here while I go have a chat with Mr. Con."

As he was closing the door, Mom called after him, "Fred, don't you lay a hand on that man. It can't be resolved that way."

Dad shook his head in silent agreement and kept right on going.

He returned about an hour later as we were beginning to eat. He quietly hung up his raincoat and as he took his place at the supper table he handed me a ten-dollar bill. He nodded towards it as he sort of whispered, "That's all I could get out of the old son-of-a-bitch."

By that time Mom had a comment about it as she shook her head and said, "Makes you wonder how many others we missed at Nuremberg."

Con never did settle up that account other than to offer me the exclusive right to hunt and trap on his land, which I accepted. Why not? There was a lot of it and it was some of the best pheasant and duck ground around there.

Sometime later, Grandad, the retired U.S. banker, reminisced about my experience for me and said, “If you ever get into the banking business, you are going to meet a lot more farmers just like him, and after you deal with a few, it won’t bother your conscience a single whit when you have to foreclose on their farms.”

In all of the years since, I have owned many guns but not one of them has ever been an 1897 or 1912 shotgun. Strange. And also, those were the only times I was hooked or hooked myself on those digging contracts.

Most of my contracts and handshake deals were not for ditches and post holes but rather for septic tanks that were becoming the norm then. Before and during the war years, most of the rural communities in Surrey still used outdoor privies. My family did right to the end. But the newer generation was more sophisticated and wanted indoor plumbing and septic tanks, which meant big holes, and this suited me just fine. I became pretty good at estimating the time a job would take and convincing the landowners that they had built their houses on a rockpile, which meant that the contract price had to be higher, usually resulting in a higher profit for the pick and shovel man.

The job and profit didn’t always stop when the hole was dug. I became involved in the business of making sure the things worked after the tanks were in place. You had to have a “starter” inside the tank to make a good brew that would keep on working the juices for a long time. It cost money to have a tank pumped out, which was necessary if the tank’s innards quit working or never started working. There were two starters, one of them known from ancient times as the surefire way of making a tank work (it could work in an outdoor privy too). Almost everybody started with the cheap, less reliable system, a solution of yeast mixed with sugar and warm water, but when that one refused to start things working, people fell back on the old reliable. Have you ever heard of, or used, a dead cat in a septic tank? If not, take it from an old expert that it works, at least most of the time. And if you don’t want to take my word for it, there were dozens of people all over south Surrey who knew about this solution before I did, so I needed no advertising to get into the midnight dead cat business. I didn’t need to make any added investment to get into it either, because

I already had the tools that were used for other covert operations—a trapping licence, a bicycle, and sometimes a .22 that could speed up results.

The system was so well known there was never any customer that would settle for using a dead dog or a dead rabbit. It had to be a cat. It seemed strange that only a cat would do, and personally, I was always somewhere in the middle, but when it came to money, the only thing those people would pay for was a cat. With that being the case, I became involved in the supply business. Please don't jump to the conclusion that I went around plugging all the neighbour's cats, because I didn't have to. The major supply came from the recently built King George Highway. When the war was over and the speed limit was freed up, lots of cats were not told about it and they were getting pancaked frequently. Hardly anyone who needed a dead cat wanted to be seen out on the highway scooping one up and carrying it home. Fortunately there are people who don't care what the neighbours think and who, for enough money, will do many strange things to help their neighbours. After all, that's what neighbours are for, isn't it?

There are supply problems to any business, and in this one sometimes (too many times) there was a wide spread of time between the market need and the splats on the highway. I often wished that my folks could afford a deep freeze. But out of dire necessity and for a consideration of larger bills, there was sometimes a way around that supply problem. This was where the midnight part came in. There were so many customers who acted squeamish about it that when the time came they wanted to be conveniently someplace else and not be told how or what happened or even look down the hole to check out what was down there. That's what is known as trust.

There was a business agent for some of these deals, and he conveniently owned a store where people came to arrange other things of a lighter nature. One time when I was in there sitting on a box having a cola, I heard him quietly tell what must have been a potential client as he nodded towards the box I was sitting on, "That's him right there. His prices are high, although I can assure you that his contracts are reliable." When you were thirteen, did your neighbours offer bouquets like that about you?

CHAPTER 7

TORPEDOMEN

Growing up on a stump farm in Surrey during the mid to late 1940s wasn't as dull and uninteresting as some people today think it was. It was anything but. Of course I'm remembering mostly my own experiences and using them as an example, which might not be all that fair to the majority of kids who grew up within the constraints of what was considered to be the right and normal way. When a person reflects for a few moments it's easy to note that most people, whether they are kids or something else, do not want to be known as abnormal. There are a few exceptions to that theory, but not many. And then when two of the exceptions get together, interesting things can develop. There are lots of descriptive words for these people, such as imaginative, innovative, and things like that.

But all it meant was some of us had wits of sorts and we used them to entertain ourselves because we knew that few other people were going to do it for us. Let's take, for instance, the time two enterprising young hunters skipped school for a few days so they could lard up their families' dinner tables with duck meat. One was twelve and the other was thirteen, but don't let that fool you because they were both big, well-fed, country kids. And big bodies make for big, sharp minds too, right? Of course it's right.

The season was half over, which meant that the surviving ducks were extremely wary and the shooting had not been successful, so the boys were beginning to wander farther afield looking for better opportunities. On one of their explorative forays they located an almost full case of CIL dynamite in a wooden box that a farmer had cached in a ditch near the end of a field. It was not a wise place to leave such stuff lying around and furthermore, according to the age of the footprints in the mud, it appeared that the farmer had probably forgotten where he had left this box. These boys decided to do the farmer a favour and keep him out of trouble with the law by packing the box up the hill and re-caching it deep in a salmonberry patch where it would be much safer. No snooping kid in his right mind would ever think of crawling into a place like that.

This was not a case of "kids playing with dynamite" in the true sense, as the father of the younger of these boys had been a powderman for the local farmers when it came to blowing stumps, and this kid had accompanied his father many times while he was doing it. The kid had a sharp eye that had observed every move his Dad made while packing, charging, and firing those charges. The kid had even been trained about where and how to dig holes under the stumps so they could be lifted with the least amount of powder, because the stuff was expensive, like around five dollars per case. The father had said many times within earshot that his kid seemed to have a natural knack for feeling out stumps that way. So what the father had done, either deliberately or accidentally, was train an authority on the subject. This world had just acquired another well-trained dynamiter.

So what do you do when you stumble into a bonanza like that? The boys knew that the dynamite had cash value, but if they found a buyer and sold it, it would feel a little bit like stealing, and as the farmer who had forgotten it was a family friend, it did not seem like a neighbourly thing to do to him. They left the powder for a few days and went back to their original project of acquiring more ducks. They didn't have much luck, even though there were lots of ducks around, especially out on the long sand bars of the Nicomekl River where they were able to stay safely out of range of anything less than an anti-aircraft gun. Or a cannon, or a mortar, or a bomb. Or a TORPEDO-MINE. With minds like those two boys had, why hadn't they thought of this obvious idea days earlier?

They were sitting in a duck blind on the dike when they sparked the idea, and right on that spot the entire plan was hatched out. There was over half a roll of white blasting fuse in the powder box, so all they needed was some blasting caps. Every farmer in the area kept a box or two stored in a shed somewhere and it took only a single day to locate a few caps that weren't being used. From there on the boys were in the business seriously. With the expertise of the younger and the boldness of the elder, things fell into place rapidly.

The plan was to borrow a boat, probably from Bill Hadden, find a small log that wasn't waterlogged, tie some loaded sticks of dynamite to it, light the fuse, and then let the mine float down in among the ducks. What could be simpler? It could be done so easily even a dumb kid could do it. Those ducks, even the big green-headed mallards that thought they were so smart, were as good as in the bag. But to be on the safe side, the boys decided to do this job scientifically, floating an unloaded log past the ducks so they could be sure how long it took to get there and how close to the ducks the river and tide would take it.

They spent the next three days getting everything arranged and practised out because they knew the explosion might attract some unwanted attention that could make it strictly a one-time event or, at best, only once in a long time. Getting the boat was no problem as the Haddens didn't seem to be needing it then and anyway, they had a couple more. The log turned out to be a better tool when it became a twelve-foot plank torn off the old Johnson Road Bridge that was already condemned. Everybody else in the area was borrowing boards off of it, so the boys felt no remorse about being no different than the rest of the river-rats.

When everything was brought together, the first thing they decided to do was test out the unloaded plank, which had been named and was thereafter referred to as "the torpedo." They floated that plank past the ducks at least six times until they knew exactly where in the river it had to be launched and how high or low the water had to be to make the timing consistent. Even the ducks and a few seagulls got into the act. After the third float-by, a few of those big, fat, foxy mallards swam out to the plank, climbed on, and rode it almost down to the King George Highway Bridge where the torpedomen took possession of it again and towed it back upriver for another trial run.

Once the running of the torpedo was understood, the torpedomen went back to shore and experimented with fuse lengths. It seemed like the stuff might have been intended to burn at a rate of about twelve inches per minute, but the experts also learned that its burning time was not consistent. The younger expert already knew something about that problem as his Dad had taught him that black powder fuse can be dangerous to use. It has a reputation for going into a smoulder, which results in a delayed action fire and sometimes no fire at all, which he referred to as a dud. When it came to those duds, the father had taught his son never to go near one until the next day. Even then, for double safety's sake he never dug out a charge but rather laid another smaller one right beside it and tried again. That pupil was observant and is still alive in 1998. So from all of their accumulated knowledge, the torpedomen decided on a five-foot fuse and two sticks of dynamite.

The next thing on the agenda was to decide the best time to perform this deed. They chose noon on a midweek day when there would be less chance of other duck hunters nosing around. The farmers in the area would be bellied up to their tables about then too, so with just a smidgen of luck the boys would have the river to themselves for at least an hour. They knew within a minute or two how long it would take the torpedo to float down before it did its stuff, but the real unknown was how many ducks they could expect to get and how long it would take to retrieve them. There were so many ducks perched on that bar during middays that it was impossible to count them, but as many as fifty or more swam out to and around the torpedo. So if all continued to go according to plan, they expected to get between fifty and a hundred ducks. That's a lot of ducks, and they realized there was going to be a problem retrieving so many. It would probably take two coal sacks to hold them all, but that was no problem because they had the coal sacks at home.

So the big day finally arrived. They forgot to attend school that Wednesday morning, and as they were getting everything lined up and ready for the noon-hour event, which they agreed might still attract a certain amount of attention, the elder suggested that since this operation was going to be so fast and easy, maybe after they loaded all the ducks into the boat and cached it they should return to school, just to be sure no suspicion was cast their way. He referred to his plan as an alibi. But the younger put in the nix for that plan as it was turning out to be a beautiful day and why spoil it? After all, a person could go to school anytime there was nothing better to do.

There are always last-minute changes to plans like these, and it was the younger who suggested that just to be doubly certain they got enough ducks, they should increase the charge to five sticks. The elder, not to be outdone, nodded in agreement as he increased it to seven sticks. He said seven was for luck. As if they might be needing it. Considering that they had lots of fuse, the expert decided to override the luck bit and used one of the new sticks to load up a second fuse and detonator. They put the charge into a small wooden box nailed to the centre of the torpedo, tacked on a lid, and then coiled both fuses on top of the lid where they would not fall into the water. The elder owned a wristwatch that soon revealed it was time to set the plan in motion.

The younger took to the oars, the elder pushed the boat and torpedo off, and the pair were off for sure. They towed the torpedo along by a short rope and they were soon out into position, perhaps two hundred yards above the sand bar. They could see the ducks from there and there were lots of them. The oarsman swung the boat around so it was facing upriver and he began giving just enough effort to the oars to hold the boat in position while the torpedoman lit the fuses, then gave the torpedo a shove and it was launched, heading straight and true, exactly as planned. Have you ever noticed what a nice feeling it is when long-thought-out plans actually work as they are supposed to? If so, you know the euphoria felt on the Nicomekl River that noon hour back in the late 1940s.

As the torpedo drifted toward its intended destination, both of the torpedomen commented on the smoke that was rising from the black powder fuses. There was enough of it that it seemed almost certain both of them were functioning properly. On down along the sand bar the torpedo cruised until it was almost up to the ducks. By this time the oarsman was letting the boat drift along at the same speed the torpedo was going, but the two were spaced about 150 yards apart so as not to spook the ducks, which seemed to know gun range within twenty yards and acted accordingly.

A strange thing happened as the torpedo cruised up to where a large group of mallards had been resting a moment before. Instead of swimming out to climb on for their customary free ride, those crazy quacks began swimming away from their destiny. Some of them even lifted off and flew down a ways ahead of the torpedo. It went on like that halfway down the bar until the elder turned to his partner and exclaimed, "It's the smoke and noise from that goddam fuse!"

In silence they both nodded in agreement. Oh, of mice and men. It was the one thing they had never thought to test for.

On the torpedo cruised. It was almost down to the end of the bar and there were only a few dumb butterball-type ducks and a few shore birds that were close enough to maybe get bagged, but the two had not planned on getting any of them. The elder began checking his watch and commented that he figured the event was about to happen almost any moment. The oarsman had been keeping pace with the torpedo even though it was obvious there were going to be few, if any, ducks to collect.

The torpedo went right by the bar and still had not blown. It was swinging out into mid-river, heading straight towards the King George Highway Bridge, which was not so very far away. Perhaps not far enough. The possible conclusion occurred to the elder first, and he asked the expert, "If that thing goes all the way to the bridge and gets hung up in those piles, do you think seven sticks is enough to blow the bridge out?"

The expert had no answer. As a matter of fact, he was beginning to have stomach and breathing problems and was even wishing he was safely back in school.

The elder stood up in the boat and exclaimed, "Wow, if we blow the bridge out it will be just like a commando raid!"

The younger was silently hoping and perhaps even praying that it wouldn't happen, because he just remembered that his mother was working that day in the Tara Supper Club, perched right up there on the hill overlooking the bridge that was about to get commandoed. The only reply the younger could croak out was, "Maybe we oughta get out of here."

Before the elder could reply to that, it was answered for both of them in a flash, KA-BOOOM, lots of smoke, flying wood, and four birds that fell out of the air into the water. The elder got knocked down into the bottom of the boat, though he wasn't hurt.

The charge had fired about 150 yards above the bridge, so no damage was done to it. It was quickly noted that three northbound cars had stopped right in the middle of the bridge and people were climbing out and looking down at the water and maybe at the torpedomen too. But that boat was heading back upriver as fast as the oarsman could lay into those oars. The boys never did go back to salvage the four unlucky birds as they doubted that anybody would want to eat them anyway. Can you imagine what two brace of seagulls would taste like?

CHAPTER 8

BABY-SITTER

When a person remembers what it was like being a pre-teen or teenager in the 1940s, it's surprising how often recollections of pennilessness take precedence over lighter and more enjoyable thoughts. Of course money is nice to think about, especially when a person does not have much or has none, as was often the case for the kids of our generation. The older we became, the more money became an obsession. It divided dreams and reality. The dreams were never-ending and always rewarding, but the reality was that there was little money to be had, especially for our age group. Most acreages were owned by families that had kids who were expected to cut their own lawns, fill the woodpiles, clean cow barns, and help with the gardens for no financial reward. Some parents bombarded their kids with messages like "You have to make yourself useful" and "It's about time you started paying your own way through this world." There were even a few parents who would locate a job for their kids and then collect their wages for them. It was legal then; perhaps it still is, but I doubt it.

In a few families, especially the ones with too many kids, there was no such thing as a "children's allowance." It was never that way in my family; any money we could acquire was always our own to spend, and if I got any I knew where to spend it! My older sister Yvonne had a different attitude towards life than I did, as from her first jobs she bought a new radio for the house and a used piano for the same. And she earned that money at the teenage rates of twenty-five to forty cents per hour. By comparison, as mentioned around here before, the first time I ever accumulated dollars they were used to buy a shotgun. To supply the family table of course.

That piano Yvonne bought brings back curious memories because my mother and sisters thought it would be a great idea if I learned to play it, and somebody even paid a neighbour woman to come and try to teach me. Yes, pay to teach me to play a piano. And this was at a time when money in our house was still as scarce as hen's teeth. Can you imagine me as a piano player?

My biggest financial problem after age twelve, when Dad let me buy that shotgun, was keeping the thing fed. It turned out to have a voracious appetite that could only be appeased with money. The shells for it came in three price ranges. There were Canucks that cost $2.25 per box of twenty-five and were best used for target practice or easy-to-kill birds like pheasants and grouse. Then there were the midrange loads called Maxims that poor people used on everything, priced at $2.60. Then there were the high-brassed and purple-coloured ones called Imperials that the plutocrats and show-offs used. They cost $3.10. Some years, when the price of spuds or milk was high, even some of the farmers could be seen carrying Imperials in their shell vests, which were becoming another show-off article. The hired help, whenever they could afford any type of shells, carried theirs in their pockets out of sight.

For a young fellow like me, it took a full day's paid labour to buy a single box of shot-shells, and this made novice hunters become accurate marksmen in a hurry or they became very hungry ones. With a shortage of both shells and money, I admit to finding one practical solution. Personally, I became an expert "sluicer," something no self-respecting hunter ever wants his best friends to see him doing. It means shooting birds on the ground or water to be sure of hitting them, rather than shooting them out of the air as those newfangled city types claimed they did (this is also called "giving the birds a sporting chance"). Later on I learned to do that too, but most of my river ducks were lined up on the water and bowled over several to a shot. I'm still not above doing it. So far, my record is eight with one shot.

For a kid with a shotgun, the cost of ammo had a financial effect on your sweet tooth. Remember that back then kids were expected to buy their own pop, ice cream (we sometimes made ours), and chocolate bars with their own money. Once in a while on special occasions, when our parents had an extra dollar, they provided such treats, but that was seldom enough that when it did happen it was very much appreciated and remembered for a long time afterwards.

So where did young money come from? Few lawns to mow for money, a few newspaper routes, and for girls there were a few baby-sitting jobs, but not many. Too many couples could barely afford the kids they had, let alone hire someone else to look after them. Small children were usually dropped off at a neighbour's or looked after by older siblings, sometimes not much older. When I think back to that and also remember that kerosene lamps were still the norm and how volatile those things were, it's amazing so many of us survived. Some parents would leave kids as young as three or four years old for long periods of time, like half a day or more, and by the time they were seven or eight, nobody even questioned the practice.

Though the practice may have been common, my hunting partner Don Turnbull and his wife Ilda did not leave their kids that way, and this responsible attitude would come to involve me. There came a time they wanted to go somewhere of an evening and could not locate a sitter for their two young boys, who were something under six years old.

It must have been a rather important occasion for the Turnbulls and they must have been desperate to go, because even though they knew me and all about me by then, they still proposed that I baby-sit their kids. When they hit me with that, I almost fell off the pop case I was sitting on in their store. ME, BABY-SIT? They acted like they were serious about the possibility of it. Even after I stopped laughing, they were both still looking expectant. I had assumed that Don was smarter than that or at least would never put pressure on his hunting partner to consider such a chore. I could not imagine a red-blooded hunter watching somebody else's kids. Their dog maybe, but not human babies. I don't know how it was with you, but this particular hunter, being the youngest in his family, could barely acknowledge the existence of kids two years younger than himself. And Don's oldest was at least six years younger. I was certain it was a joke, but from the looks on their faces it was obvious they didn't see it that way.

I forget the leverage that was used but it was probably using words like "best friend," "hunting partners," and stuff like that. I did finally agree to do it as long as they kept their mouths shut so none of my other, more sensible hunting partners heard about it. After all, there was a reputation to protect. I would have much preferred volunteering to be a second or even a first at a duel.

Ilda did promise to have the kids already put to bed before I arrived and I wouldn't even have to look at them. In turn I had to promise to get them out of the house if it caught fire. Don said I could have three free pop, read his hunting and gun books, and the real bonus was I could clean and polish all of his guns, of which he had a small arsenal. I could even sit in Don's personal chair while doing it, so there was going to be fair compensation. There was another part to this job that I didn't mind doing, and that was acting as night watchman over the business. The garage had been broken into in the past, and as Don had said many times that if he ever caught a thief in there he would ventilate him, I was just itching for the chance to do it for him with that .455 Smith & Wesson.

That night I wasn't destined to be so lucky. It was not a lucky night for one of those little Turnbull boys either.

At some point during the night as I was sitting at the table cleaning a pistol, I heard the bedroom door open and looked up to see two heads peering around the edge of it. Ilda had already told me that the boys had been told they were NOT to come out and bother me, so I decided right then and there to exert some authority. I refreshed their memories for them by roaring what must have been a believable threat about what I'd do if they came another step further. The door slammed and I neither saw nor heard a peep out of them again. I had to admit one thing about those two, and that was they were well-behaved and obedient kids. As a matter of fact, for small kids they were on the better side of average. All of the other neighbours used to say so. But the way I saw it they were still too young to be useful.

The night progressed with no burglar or anything else interesting, and when Don and Ilda returned there was nothing to report, other than for me to admit to Ilda that the kids had been no problem at all. I believe she did retort that after a few more sittings I would lose my fear of "little demons." Well, who knows, I thought. So I went home to bed and the ordeal was over. Until the afternoon of the next day, that is.

As customary, I dropped into Turnbull's store for my daily cola and to listen to the older neighbours settle up the world's affairs. I got through the door but never quite made it to the cooler. As soon as Ilda saw me she flew into a spitting rage and verbally started tearing shingles off every piece of me. She was carrying on like nothing I had ever seen from her before.

"Why didn't you let the boys go to the bathroom last night?" she screamed at me.

Ilda was normally a real pleasant lady. I didn't have a clue what she was referring to and I told her so. "Why didn't they just go?" I asked. "Aren't they toilet trained yet?"

"What do you mean, not toilet trained?" she said, almost trembling. "When Terry opened the bedroom door to come out, you hollered at them and threatened to blow their heads off if they didn't get back into bed." There was still fire in her eye. "So one of them made a mess in his bed and by God, Ted Choate, you don't seem to realize how close you came this morning to being dragged back over here and made to clean that mess up. You should have had your head and mouth shoved into it," she raged. She was really in a snit and I was feeling very alone. Nobody told me that baby-sitting could get this dangerous. My hunting partner just stood behind her with a stiff smile on his face like he was practising to be an undertaker at a wedding. He never offered a single word to help me out.

I was not used to making apologies but did try one. I was beginning to tell her what really happened, but that only brought her another step closer. She stuck her finger under my nose and almost into it. "Ted Choate, don't you dare try telling me a lie because I'll take the word of my sons over yours any day of the week!"

Have you ever tried explaining a misunderstanding to someone else's mother? Sometimes you can see that they do not want to know the truth of things. Well I didn't want to give it a try either, so beat a hasty retreat without even buying my pop.

It was several days before I conjured up enough nerve to step through that door again. But time heals all and when I did venture back to feel out the winds of war, the gale had died down. As a matter of fact, both of them were even laughing about it in their own way. On the other hand, they had not kept their word about the tight-lip part of our agreement. All the neighbours had been told every detail from a point of view that contained some exaggeration. And not a single soul wanted to hear my version of it, so there was nothing to do but let them live in their blissful ignorance.

One thing about that ordeal, though, is that it quickly restored the proper order of things. Neither the Turnbulls nor any other Elgin neighbour ever asked Ted Choate to baby-sit their kids again.

CHAPTER 9

RACCOONS

Almost every country kid goes through the stage of wanting to tame a wild animal, and most of them try it at least once. I was no exception. It's hard to understand why we insist on doing this. It could be a way of proving to ourselves that we can dominate everything in sight or perhaps we are fascinated by and attracted to the unknown things around us. It doesn't really matter why, because we are what we are, and we keep right on trying to bolster our egos at the animals' expense.

Many of them are attracted to us too, and that is surprising as we have a reputation for treating them mighty harshly, especially when you think in terms of zoos and game farms. But those places are regulated to humane standards you say? Oh, sure they are. Have you ever noticed how fast a captive wild animal takes to the bush if it's lucky enough to escape from our clutches? Even some of our more domesticated types, like house cats. Once they learn how to fend for themselves, we take our eyes and lives in our hands if we try to lay a hand on them again. When domesticated horses take to the bush for a few years and are recaught, many of them want nothing more to do with humans and they can be extremely hard to rebreak, right to the point of impossible. Even with the best of them, it's a long time before a rider should trust them as much as before they had that taste of wild freedom. I have never met a wild dog, but there are such things and the ones that are adopted by coyotes or wolves will never come to hearth again. The only thing that retames them is a jolt of long lightning.

We are even tinkering and trying to tame God down to our level too, and our success will be judged by how soon this earth is no longer wild and green. I guess we just like to see ourselves as the Lion Tamers of the Universe and even beyond.

In our family it was Mom and me that were the animal lovers mostly, although Dad and my sisters did take to dogs and cats, but neither of those girls ever learned to milk a cow and only Pat ever tried her hand at riding a horse. The chickens, rabbits, and pigs were pretty well left to my care, especially when it came time to butcher them. There were domestic trade-offs, as the girls were better gardeners than I was and after breaking a couple of Mom's prized Royal Albert tea cups, I was forever after relieved of all dishwashing and table duties. I don't remember ever having to sweep a floor. But animals of one sort or another were always in my mind and I wasn't just trying to get them to step into a trap or into my gunsight either, as my turn as the "lion tamer" arrived in due time. I have often suspected that the urge is like falling in love. It just happens, and the attraction in both cases could be the euphoria of flirting with danger. Make a mistake with the lion and you are gobbled, a mistake with the other and you die a pauper. The only way to avoid either is to keep our hands in our pockets and our pecker in our pants, but we aren't very bright and who wants to miss out on all the excitement anyway?

It was the lion tamer bug that caught me up first, and my first lions turned out to be a pair of squirrels. One was a red squirrel whose name became Daylight and the other was a nocturnal flying squirrel who took on the handle of Midnight. This was an educate-myself experiment. There were no teachers to get a start from so it was a trial and error that turned out to be mostly error. At least half of it was. The first thing I learned was I didn't know as much about squirrels as I thought I did. That was brought to light soon after I put both squirrels into the same wire cage. After three or four days of watching them, it dawned on me that I had not seen Midnight for a couple of days. I opened their nesting box that was inside the big cage, and all I found of him was his tail. Two lessons learned here, first being that red and flying squirrels do not like each other, and second, red squirrels will eat meat. Did you know that? Well, you do now.

So it was back to the bush with my homemade tin box trap to add another red to keep Daylight company. He had a name too but I can't recall it, not that it made any difference because they looked more alike than identical twins. Even after I fed them and talked to them for a couple of weeks, they became no tamer than the ones that scampered around the yard outside the cage. Dad suggested that it might have something to do with Mom's big orange tomcat, Tom Tidy, who had taken up an almost permanent residence on top of the squirrel cage. How do you stop a cat from being a cat? I couldn't figure out how to do it, so after another week I turned my lions loose to join the ones in the yard.

I still had the bug though, perhaps even moreso because I began casting thoughts and eyes onto greater dangers like foxes and deer. Dad was running true to form. He said the first time a fox looked sideways at a chicken, it would be turned into a coat collar, and if a pet deer nipped the orchard trees, it would be the soup pot for the deer. Thoughts of having a skunk deodorized surfaced too, but Dad doused them with cold water when he explained that even if I could catch one in a spray-proof trap, and even if we could find a veterinarian that would perform the operation, that vet would charge ten dollars or more for doing it. He was talking in the price range of four boxes of shotgun shells, so the skunk got finished off right then. There was still the odd cougar and bobcat being reported, but I had not yet seen either of them and was not sure if I was ready for such a sudden jump in size and danger, so Tom Tidy and Lady did not have to worry for the time being. The lion tamer urge didn't die then. It just went dormant for a while, and don't forget, where there is a will there is a way.

The urge resurfaced again when I was about thirteen and was at a weekend softball game at the Elgin schoolyard. An older kid from Sullivan, Don Grant, solved my problem. We must have been talking about hunting, trapping, and whatever else teenage boys talk about when Don mentioned that he owned a pet raccoon. Guess whose ears perked up? Even though I had been trapping for several years, I had still never seen, much less trapped, a raccoon as they were not very numerous in our area. There were always a few tracks along the low edge of tidewater on the rivers, but the trackmakers were extremely wary to the point of being phantoms. They were listed on the Vancouver Fur Sale auction newsletters, though their fur value was not high, only a small notch above skunks.

Don Grant had an interesting theory about their value as he explained that because they were quite easy to tame and interesting to live around, their live value should be higher than their dead one. For instance, a dead coon was worth at best $1.50. Don's suggestion was that a live coon that was already half tame had to be worth at least twice as much as the other way, which brought the price up around three dollars. He also casually mentioned that he might be interested in selling the one he had, but I didn't have the three dollars, only two dollars and no immediate job in sight. I just as casually told him I figured a half-wild coon could not be worth over two dollars and asked him if he would consider it. He thought a bit and looked me over, considering the prosperity of my appearance, which luckily wasn't too impressive, and he then nodded and said, "Sure kid" (being about four years older, he always called me that). "Next Sunday you bring two dollars to the ball game and I'll bring the coon over in a gunny sack."

Don Grant seemed to know a lot about coons. He warned me not to expect the coon to act as tame as it really was because the five-mile ride in a gunny sack on the bike might leave it upset for a while. That sounded reasonable. He also went into detail about what type of pen I should make for it, with a hiding box and all that. At home we had dozens of unused rabbit cages and I explained to Don my idea of patching four of them together to allow for lots of climbing room. Don again nodded in agreement as he replied, "Yeah, sure kid, that will work great."

He seemed to have something else on his mind and it came out as he thoughtfully advised, "Say kid, there is another thing you should try and get hold of and that's a pair of heavy leather gloves because if your coon gets chased by a dog or something, it can become real wild, like a crazy cat, only a coon is stronger and has bigger teeth and claws, and without gloves for protection you might not be able to hold it. A pair of welding gloves are about right," he added. The only pair of welding gloves I had ever seen belonged to a good friend of mine and I doubted if he would part with them, but I still had a week to cross that bridge.

During the evenings of the following week, I worked like a beaver to join eight rabbit cages together, complete with a meshed-in walkway between them, a sunken basin with a garden hose so my raccoon could have continuous running water, and a nice deep hiding box with a lid so I could clean it out once in a while. I have never been the world's best carpenter, but that coon pen was probably my life's best effort.

One evening when I was busy in there, Dad walked by and came over to watch and asked me what I was up to. He had not yet been told my plan as I knew he liked surprises, but it was time to begin softening him up, so I told him the truth: that I had located a den of raccoons and planned to catch one and bring it home alive. He stood there watching me for a while and as he started walking away he left me with a remark that was almost expected, "Well, if your raccoon trapping is on par with your fox trapping, I guess the rabbits and chickens won't have too much to worry about." As a parting shot he added, " I sure wish you would put as much effort into the saw handle as you do to these other harebrained schemes of yours." Even though it was tempting to offer a wager as to the possible success of my coon catching, I decided to let him get away with it as part of the "softening up" angle, because there was a slight chance it would be needed. It turned out to be a wise decision too.

Don Grant was true to his word, as he showed up at the Sunday ball game with a young raccoon in a gunny sack. Our deal was finalized as all the neighbourhood kids looked on and into the sack that had a very angry coon spitting back at them. From his immediate defiance, I sensed I had finally found my lion and an appreciative audience that went with it. There was one kid in particular, Norman Hadden, who out of what I figured was pure jealousy commented when he looked into the sack, "You know, there is some sort of saying about those things and it has something to do with being 'as lousy as a pet coon.' I wonder if this one is?"

Don Grant set that smart mouth straight in a hurry, perhaps fearing a lost sale, as he stood a little straighter and looked Norm in the eye and informed him, "If that coon is lousy then so am I." Don was much bigger than Norm and Norm was not the stupidest kid around, so the question was answered without need of further discussion.

There was no ball game for me that day because with lion in the sack I lit out for home. By the time we arrived the coon had been named. With a face and tail like that he could only be Daniel Coon (with full respects to Daniel Boone intended), which was later shortened to Danny. There didn't seem to be any need to inform Mom and Dad about the addition to the family as they were becoming used to my trapping successes and didn't show much interest. There was still a strong possibility that more propaganda time was needed, so I kept Danny to myself for a while.

When he was first released into his new home, he reared up like a bear as he gave me a good spitting and hissing to, and then he went straight to the sunken water basin and washed his hands and face. Next he made a thorough check of the enclosure and a frequent inspection of me as I was sitting quietly inside with him. These usually ended up with another good round of spitting opinions from him to me. He did act half tame all right, but Don had warned me not to try picking him up until the coon said he was ready for it, and the size of his fangs made it an easy decision to go along with this advice.

The coon pen's first visitors came almost immediately and were Rusty, my Irish setter hunting partner, and Tom Tidy, Mom's tomcat. Rusty did not appreciate my being in the pen with Danny, but he soon ignored the coon. It was different with the cat. When Tom and Danny spotted each other, they both ran up to the wire-mesh fence that separated them and went through all sorts of interesting-to-watch tantrums. The cat had more faith in that wire than I did, because that coon was threatening deadly mayhem and looked more like he could deliver than the cat could, even though the cat was noisier about displaying his own doubtful abilities. One of their most hilarious exhibitions was trying to out-puff each other. Tom Tidy could make himself look like he belonged on a witch's broom, but the coon outdid him every time and the pogo-stick-style dance that went with it was more impressive than the cat's arched back.

As time went on the three animals became fairly good friends, though the coon was always the boss. All animals with tails seem to be sensitive about them and proud, and that used to get the cat into embarrassing situations when the coon was loose. There was nothing in this world pleased that coon more than sneaking up on the cat from behind, clamping both hands around the cat's tail, and watching the tail slide through his grip. That usually was accompanied by a loud screech from the cat, which just added to Danny's delight. They attracted human attention with that act when it happened inside the house, and Mom would broom Danny out the door, an indignity he did not appreciate. But it was always worth whatever price it cost him, because when he was loose that cat dared not sleep. Strange thing about that though, in all of the years they shared our lives with us, I never once saw them get into an actual fight. As for the coon and the dog, they always tended to ignore each other, although Rusty would occasionally growl at Danny when he thought the coon was becoming a little too familiar, like checking out Rusty's tail. When the coon was close, the dog learned not to wag it so much. But they too never fought.

That must have been a busy summer for my parents because Danny was home for several days before they became aware of him. It had always been my job to milk the cow and then deliver the full bucket to Mom at the house, where she would strain and separate it. One of those evenings I must have been careless with my secrecy because she spotted me scooping out a tobacco-can-full of fresh milk and heading out the door with it, and she called after me, "Where are you going with that?"

"Oh, I've been feeding Tom Tidy out at the rabbitry so he will stay out there and catch more mice," I informed her as I kept right on moving out.

Who knows why, but she must have sensed something was up because as I finished pouring the milk into Danny's dish, her voice behind me jolted me into a higher state. "What have you got in there?"

"Oh, just my friend Danny," was the truthful reply.

"Why, you've got a damn raccoon in there!" she needlessly reminded me.

"Well, I've been telling everybody that I was going to catch a live coon to tame and train," I defended in a hurry, which was the almost truth.

The conversation went back and forth that way for a few minutes. All the while Danny was lapping up the pure Jersey cream. When he was finished he still had a lot of it spread all over his face, which he proceeded to wash off with his hands. In the past few days he had tamed down fast, so he was sitting in my lap while he was doing it and he was purring like a little motorboat. It was still him that set the pace of our relationship and even though he was climbing all over me, I was not yet allowed to hold him. That would come in his good time and as time went on, for a dish of milk and especially cream, that coon would do almost anything.

Mom was still standing there watching us. As she turned to go she commented, "Well he sure is a cute little fellow, but you had better tell Dad about him tonight and you had also better figure out a way to convince him that your Danny is not going to kill our rabbits or the neighbour's chickens, because I do know that they have a bad reputation that way. And they are supposed to love eggs too."

There was one single word from that conversation that was glowing through my mind, that little four-letter word "cute." As soon as she said it I knew we had her in the bag. And that being the case, when Dad came home to face the reality, no matter what he might think to himself, he would have to follow suit as he was never anywhere near a match for mother's temper or persuasion. That single word, when it comes from a woman, has the strength of a marriage vow, so Danny had just become family.

The lion tamer was to learn many things from his new charge, and it was probably the best education there is as after a while we have to acknowledge that wild animals have much more to teach us than we have to teach them. It is interesting to observe and work with them, and the single word that describes all aspects of the relationship (and there will be no progress until the human side is prepared to concede it) is "unpredictable." Other words to remember are "perseverance and persuasion" without temper, because wild animals cannot be tamed by force. Not if we want to trust them they can't be, because there are many recorded cases of larger animals biding their time and taking bloody revenge. Wild animals have an obvious dignity and this must be acknowledged. Sometimes they will accommodate human silliness, but only if you can persuade them it's in their own best interest to do so, and that usually comes with a lot of carrot and little, if any, stick.

Don Grant had been right about Danny being at least half tame because week by week I was able to take more liberties with him without being warned off. He never did like to be held for long, usually just long enough to be picked up and hoisted onto my shoulder, and that became one of his favourite methods of travel. Once up there he would place one hind foot on each of my shoulders, drape himself forward over the top of my head, and use my hair to hang on with as we wandered about. I thought that was a pretty neat thing as it gave me my own unique and very much alive Daniel Coon hat. It could get dicey when a stranger or strange dog came near, as Danny would start digging in, preparing to do battle from my head and shoulders. He learned to trust me for defence. It took him just a short while to appreciate the fact that I was on his side, which he first witnessed from a tree perch as I threw rocks at the dogs. I cannot remember throwing rocks at human strangers, but he did learn to come to me if he sensed danger from them. As that raccoon got older and bigger, he would not back down from a single dog or human. He would actually go after the dogs, mostly because of their tails. The strange thing was that even though he was fascinated by tails on other animals, nobody, not even me, was ever permitted to touch his. But around our own yard, as Rusty and Tom Tidy could attest, Danny Coon loved tail.

Another of his favourite pastimes was playing with a running garden hose. He used to spend days on end trying to figure out how to stop the water from coming out. He conjured up every way a coon could to sneak up on that thing, he pounced on it and then tried various methods of clamping his teeth and hands over the nozzle, but nothing ever worked. He always got squirted. Sometimes when I was playing with him as he wrestled with that hose, I shut the tap off. Did that ever make him happy. He would go into one of his pogo-stick dances without the puffing up out of pure ecstasy. Just as he began calming down and prepared to go to sleep and dream of his victory, I would turn the hose back on. We even saw him try to bury that hose, and a few times he tried using his weight and sat on it. There are people who preach that animals have no imagination, but the truth is, when humans finish themselves off around here, coons may take over the world.

Some men are chastised for having inquiring hands, but they have only a fraction of the curiosity of raccoon hands. In Danny's case, anything that was hollow or looked hollow he had to check out right up to shoulder length, and there was hardly anything that pleased him more than emptying out a flower vase, usually by tipping it over first. That usually brought him into direct action with Mom's broom. Danny learned to hate brooms and when he found one that wasn't being used, he would shred it, hence another brooming and banishment to his pen for several days. That didn't save the next broom, because his memory and opinion of them was lifelong and he had the persistence of Job.

One of his favourite treats was small-sized dog biscuits. I used to carry a few in my shirt pocket. When I sat in a particular old stuffed chair, Danny would immediately climb up on the back of it and drape himself over my shoulder where he purred by the hour and combed my hair with his fingers. First, though, he would lean over my shoulder and check out all my shirt pockets for those biscuits. I often teased him by buttoning the pocket shut, which was frustrating for him as he lost time figuring out how to undo those buttons. That frustration could make his play a little rough and it cost me a few torn shirts and light scratches on my chest.

One day a young woman came to visit Mom. She plopped into my chair, which was okay until I came out of my bedroom with Danny in trail. The woman was quite taken with him so I put him through a few paces and it turned out Danny was taken with the woman, too. He hopped up on the back of the chair and proceeded to comb her hair, which she thought was just hilarious. Danny always was a good performer, especially when he sensed people appreciated it. He spotted that the woman had a pocket on her blouse, so he immediately went fishing for a biscuit. I never did find out what he discovered in there, but whatever it was would not come out easily, so he went after it with both hands and part of his reward was a shriek from the woman as she tried to tear loose from the chair and raccoon. Danny held on until there was another torn shirt and a red-faced woman who was trying to hold it in place. His next reward was another brooming from Mom, who almost gave me the same as she told me to, "Get that damn coon out of this house and don't you ever bring him back in here again." She only meant part of it, as Danny was back without comment from her within a few days. Even though I was old enough to be curious in my own right, nobody ever told me what Danny found or if any other damage was done, so my teenage imagination had to suffice.

Mother often told people that she figured Danny's mentality was the equivalent of a two-year-old boy's. That being the case, we had to "kid proof" parts of the house. For instance, all lower cupboards had to have button closures replaced with stiff hook-and-eye affairs, and long curtains were no longer in vogue in our house. It was not wise to leave some types of food on the table, either. Danny was accidentally locked in the house alone a couple of times and rather than go into needless detail here, I'll leave you to imagine what the house looked like on our return. Whatever you come up with will be about what it was. That led to another brooming and banishment to the cage for a week or so. It must have been worth it though, because next time into the house he went straight to the cupboards that he remembered had the most interesting goodies. By that time they were locked and he never did figure out the hook-and-eye rigs or the spring-loaded latches.

The older he got, the less he liked his fancy cage. This became an annoying situation for him and me as bedtime for humans was wake-up time for coons. They are as nocturnal as a cat. When Danny sensed it was about time for him to be locked up for the night, he would locate the biggest fir tree in our yard and up he would go. All the way up. And there he would stay, only sometimes coming down for a saucer of cream. Usually he spent the entire night up there or somewhere more interesting until hunger or just plain goodies brought him to ground, to house, to cage again. There were times that he was absent for a few days, but he always came home eventually. One thing that drove him home was being treed by a pack of loose dogs. Sometimes I located him by listening for a pack of barking, howling dogs. After I dispersed them, Danny would slide right down and willingly accept his ride back home on my shoulders. He did learn that I would protect him, and when those dogs chased him or if he became frightened by something else, he would run to his cage or my bedroom window if he could.

When I knew he was gone for the night, rather than go look for him I learned to leave my bedroom window open, as his preferred place of residence had become my bed. Not on it—in it, especially if I was in it too. Mom was never pleased with that situation, as a few times when Danny arrived back home to my bedroom when I was away, he became protective of my bed to the point that he chased Mom out of the bedroom. He was a clean coon, though, except when he arrived in the bedroom from one of his fishing forays in the nearby creek, and then his muddy feet brought comment from Mom on washdays. At times like that he was not the greatest bed partner either, or when he made a midnight arrival from out of a rainstorm. A soaking wet coon sliding into your bed in the middle of the night makes for a shocking awakening. And whether he arrived that way or dry and agreeable, he was persistent about demanding the centre part of the bed. Sometimes when I tried to push him to his own side he would challenge me with a hiss or growl, and as my naked body felt vulnerable under those conditions, he usually ended up having his way. Have you ever tried sleeping with a half-wild coon? If not, I recommend you give it some critical thought before you do, because the danger of accidentally rolling on top of the coon can turn you into a light sleeper—or it better had.

One thing that absolutely got Danny evicted from the bedroom or the entire house was his farting. God, how such a small animal could store that much gas without exploding eludes explanation. This was almost always brought on by his successful expeditions fishing for spawned-out salmon in the creek. He could eat a ten- or twelve-pound salmon in one sitting and for the next three days, look out. That was a problem because after a feast like that was when he most wanted to come inside and curl up and go to sleep for a couple of days. If he went into hiding in that condition, he damn soon gave himself away and when he did, even I wanted him OUT.

It was from these many observations and shared experiences that I became the local lion-taming coon expert. Even as I spent time with Danny, the reality of life always came back to that money problem, which meant I was continuously conjuring up ideas to make more of it, preferably honestly as outright stealing was not in fashion unless it was from a bank. Even though I was able to earn more money digging holes or working on the local farms, trapping was my preferred way of doing it, but the season was only three months long and no matter how hard I tried, I was never able to ration the trapping income across the nine intervening months. It seldom lasted much beyond the first one.

It must have been about a year after getting Danny that a couple of events and a brainstorm resulted in a new business or at least an extension of the old one. Don Grant's theory that "live coons should be worth more than dead ones" kept coming back to me, especially after Danny joined our family. Just thinking of how close Danny must have come to becoming a pelt instead of the most interesting of friends created unsettling feelings, and it was during one of those philosophical moments that the mental lights began flashing.

The first event that led to this sparking was my building myself an eleven-foot rowboat that allowed me to begin ranging almost the full length of the Nicomekl River. The second event was my discovery, near the upper end of the river, of the tracks of what had to be a colony of raccoons. I located these coons in early summer, so fur trapping was out of the question, but if Don Grant could convince me that live coons were worth money, why couldn't I convince others of the same? All I needed was more live coons to lion tame. Why not? I had the boat, the knowledge of how to catch them, the proven ability to tame a raccoon, and the big boost of having Danny to help me gain the trust of completely wild ones. All of this could be turned into an off-season cash flow, especially since I had discovered coons are far more active in summer than during the cold months. Not only could the lion-tamed wild ones be sold, but if the right combination came out of a live trap, with Danny's help there could be fully domesticated coons born and raised right alongside the rabbits. There might be a fortune to be made.

When I told Mom and Dad about my new proposal, neither one of them rose up very high to the idea and they began laying down a whole bunch of new ground rules that were completely unnecessary. This time nobody doubted my ability to add more coons, but no new ones were going to be allowed to become family, as Mom said our house and bodies could not withstand the impact. How does anybody know a thing like that if it's not tried? In situations like this, the best method of persuasion was the old tried and proven "parents respond best after the fact" strategy, so that became the game plan. Actually I do not think Mom or Dad really thought they had made me a believer in their rules and when they watched me build and experiment with a large box trap in the yard, they appeared to accept, though rather glumly, what fate might drop on their doorstep.

My first task was to invent and build a box trap that would not only work, but would also hold the coon after it was caught. After commandeering another wire rabbit hutch and reinforcing it, I began experimenting with a sliding trapdoor that was attached to a simple "pull-down" trigger system. Another kid, Jimmy Mann, and I scientifically tested the trap by baiting it and then catching and recatching Tom Tidy, Danny, and Jimmy's small dog. The cage and trapdoor worked perfectly on all of the animals, and only the cat became hyped up about being caged. By the third time the trapdoor sprang shut behind Danny, he never even looked up but simply kept eating the bait. When it was finished, he was ready to start all over again. Coons are so smart.

Everything was going just as planned, so Jimmy helped me carry the trap to the river and load it into the boat. From there on, I was on my own. I had sworn Jimmy to secrecy on this operation because if it turned out to be as successful as it appeared it would be, I did not want a lot of competition coming in sideways and stealing the business. I had seen ads in U.S. magazines offering tame raccoons for twenty dollars, so the probability that I had finally stumbled into something good was almost beyond doubt. I believe this is called either speculation or delusion depending on if it's being described before or after the event.

The long row upriver the following day to set the trap was enjoyable work, as pleasurable as planting a money tree. Summer trapping is a lot easier than winter trapping. For instance, I don't know how the Nicomekl is today, but in the late 1940s there were many places along the river where a person could stop and go swimming without the encumbrance of a bathing suit. I had done it a few times in the winter, too, but never deliberately and you can safely believe me when I say that summer immersion is better by far.

The trap was large, probably four feet long by two feet wide and eighteen inches high, and must have weighed around sixty pounds. There was no way to camouflage a trap that size, but raccoons from around the Langley-Surrey border were not wary of things like wire enclosures. They had a bandit reputation of raiding chicken and rabbit cages, so they would have no particular fear of walking into this one for something as tempting as a piece of rotten fish.

It took to the fourth day before the trap was sprung, but what was looking out at me was a very angry black tomcat, not a cuddly coon. He sure acted like one of the wild types. At that time there was an English fur buyer in the Lower Mainland who was paying a dollar per for the winter pelts of wild domestic cats, but this being summer, this fellow's black hide was worth nothing. After getting rid of him, I reset the trap. Four more coonless rows up the river suggested that there might have to be a change of plans. These wild cousins of Danny were certainly aware of the trap by week's end, as there were coon tracks all around it, but for some reason they were refusing to co-operate. Perhaps fish was not the best coon bait after all. It was one of Danny's favourite foods, but it occurred to me it might be something he became educated to, like the dog biscuits. And then one day while rowing home it finally dawned on me. Coons are not used to going into cages to steal fish. They go in looking for chickens. That had to be the answer.

By that time there were only about a dozen of our original White Leghorn chickens that were still tame enough to come home to roost and lay eggs. I wasn't foolish enough to take one of those, and I didn't want to go hunting for a wild one that would cost a shotgun shell or two. A couple of our neighbours had lots of chickens and an expensive habit of forgetting to pen them up at night. At that time the major chicken thieves were not coons but mostly dogs and cats. So that night the Askerbergs donated a chicken to the cause and by noon of next day it was hanging in the coon trap. Dead of course.

Four more days of steady rowing saw more coon tracks on the outside of the trap and one more cat on the inside. A grey one this time. Something was still not quite right and again it was while rowing home that enlightenment got jolted into an upgrade. Rowing boats must be a good mental exerciser, because over the years it is surprising how often my education was advanced while I was doing it. Perhaps that's why many famous people spent so much time fishing.

This time the revelation was that coons don't go into pens looking for dead chickens. They like those nice, squawky, live ones. So that night while Charlie Creer and his friend Sandy were having a party, Charlie donated a big, brown, noisy chicken to the cause of reducing the wild chicken thief population. Next morning, after the umpteenth coonless row upriver, Chicken and I arrived at the site where I did a fast carpentry job inside the trap. It ended up with a twelve-inch wire-mesh cage at the doorless end, a nice cosy place for Chicken to live for a day or so. Even with the addition of water and more food than she needed, Chicken did not seem to be well-disposed towards her new surroundings and she gave me loud comment about it, but that was her fate regardless.

And that was exactly the formula that worked. The next day when I arrived, Chicken had a cage partner consisting of one angry raccoon. Surprisingly, Chicken was still alive but terrified to muteness. First things first, and because Chicken had been reluctantly co-operative she was released and never seen again. One of my other trapping tools came into play then. This was the big coal sack with a drawstring top that I used to release live dogs and cats when they got caught in the steel traps and snares. I soon received new information and that was there is a great deal of difference between sacking an almost-willing dog or cat and an unwilling wild coon. This coon was angry and he was bigger than Danny and stronger too, and the size of his teeth gave a person pause as he thought about how to handle the new situation. This coon's ears-laid-back anger was a lot different to Danny's huffs and bluffs, and this fellow acted as though he might be short on bluff.

It took two hours of prodding with a stick and other comparable persuasions before that coon finally gave up and tried to escape through the dark sack. I believe that he was as exhausted as I was, because when he got in there and the drawstring made sure he was staying, he lay quietly in the bottom of the boat. Some sixth sense told me that rather than reset the trap and perhaps have more than one of these animals to train, I should settle for one at a time, at least until more was known about dealing with such a bundle of determined fury. Thoughts of this general gist churned in my mind all the way downriver and I wondered, since there had already been several modifications to this new business, how many others would be needed before it settled into a routine of assured financial income? It was a good thing that I had a young, flexible mind because from then on there were no set rules and even theories had to be changed within seconds.

I had not bothered to build a separate cage for a new raccoon. I must have simply assumed all along that as Danny was as tame as a coon could be, the new wild coons would be dropped into his pen with him and he would help tame them to the first level of domesticity. Considering how intelligent coons are, I was sure they would follow Danny's lead and give me a shortcut method of taming. That theory did not work for so much as a second. The instant the new coon touched ground in Danny's cage, those two locked onto each other and did the fur ever fly. Within seconds there was blood and fur everywhere. I had to make a decision in seconds. Those two had to be separated somehow or I was going to be out of the coon business, perhaps for keeps.

The door into the coon cage was not very large, but I grabbed the coal sack and crawled in with the idea of somehow bagging one of them, but that did not work out either as just as soon as I tried pinning one down, they BOTH turned on me. Whichever one was Danny was not bluffing any more than the wild cousin was. When they both teamed up that way in the cramped enclosure, I was in trouble and decided to get my own pride to hell out of there. Just as I was almost out the door, one of those ankle-biters grabbed me by the pant leg and tripped me out flat. I was hanging half in and half out of the cage with my back end on the inside with those two snarling coons. Strange things go through a man's mind when he is stretched out that way. Then one of them landed in the centre of my back and as I ducked my head and kept trying to kick my way out the door, it jumped outside and I saw it sail up a nearby fir tree. They were both so fluffed up that it was impossible to tell who was who, as coon fights are nothing like a dog fight where you can easily keep track of your buddy. During this particular fight there were no buddies and it was every man for himself. I did finally kick free of the other coon and get out the door, and before he came out after another grip I slammed the door shut on him.

This was shaping up to be an eventful day. The caged coon and I sat there staring at each other. He did not seem to be badly hurt, other than a torn ear and a few patches of missing fur, so I figured it was Danny on the inside and began talking to him to calm him down. There were no purrs in reply, only spits, growls, and hisses, so after a few minutes I knew that the Surrey-Langley

Border Raider was still imprisoned. By this time the real Danny had come down the tree into the lower branches, but he refused to be persuaded to come to ground, so I just ignored him. He was talking to me, so it seemed highly probable that within a few hours he would come to the bedroom window and join the family again.

So now I was down to real lion taming, which meant scheming or at least outscheming the lion. I went back into the pen with the Raider. Danny's pen was made up of eight wire-doored rabbit hutches with all the doors wired open, so as soon as I entered the larger walkway between them, the new coon jumped up into one of the higher cages and offered to do battle in there. Rather than accommodate him, I slammed the two doors closed and wired them shut, and he seemed relieved that there was something between us. Relieved enough that one of his first acts was to begin drinking from a pot of water as soon as I put it in the cage. That was a positive move as every writer of all the books I had been reading about live-trapping wild animals warned that older animals will sometimes refuse food and water and actually starve themselves to death. This one had no plans of dying from thirst. So far, so good, and it seemed like it was about time that something was going according to those earlier plans.

Later in the evening, Danny's curiosity finally got the better of him. He came down from his perch and went straight into the part of his pen that was left open for him. It looked like he had it in mind to chase Wild Coon back to the bush, but I kept Wild locked into his own side of the pen and whether Danny liked it or not, that side became Wild's home.

I made another decision then too, and that was to name the new addition "Wild." The two coons were still acting hostile towards each other as there was a continuous display of huffing, puffing, and spitting, but at the same time they seemed to be extremely curious about each other. This went on for about two days and by that time I noticed that Wild was beginning to eat anything that Danny ate and was copying him to some degree. For instance, Wild had a nest or hiding box and he would hide in it when I went into the main enclosure, but if I sat there quietly and let Danny climb over me and purr, within a few minutes Wild's black nose, then his face, and then the rest of him would come out to watch us. So there was a certain amount of copycat actions and that was encouraging, but I did concede that because Wild was an adult coon there was a limit to how well he would domesticate. The lion tamers of the books were probably right when they said it was most successful when done with young animals.

I kept referring to Wild as "he," but for a few days I was still not sure and was hoping Wild might turn out to be the other way. When Dad finally discovered we had an addition in the pen, he came out to look it over and one of his observations was to assure me that I had two male coons so it was unlikely there would be any pitter-patter of little feet. What he did suggest as a probability was that male coons would not get along well together and there might even be a fight to the death, so I had better decide what was going to happen from then on. Considering that Danny already had the run of the yard and house, it did not seem fair that Wild should be condemned to total captivity for the rest of his life, so somehow I had to locate a new home for him.

There was always the danger that Wild would get loose and kill Danny or, as Mom worried, Tom Tidy or Rusty, because they were no longer used to running from a coon and that hesitation might cost them dearly. We knew that a coon was fully capable of taking on a larger animal, because when Danny met a lone dog or even a human, he often put the run on them. It was only a pack of dogs that he would run from. The two people Danny had it in for were Mom, anytime she had a broom or mop in her hand, and for some reason Grandad, as Danny went for his ankles whenever he had the opportunity. Perhaps Danny did that because he got such an interesting reaction from Grandad. For instance, one time he "treed" Grandad on the chopping block in the woodshed and another time he chased him up a ladder, and those were not the only confrontations either. When Grandad came to visit, he carried a long sticklike cane and before he entered our house he would open the door a crack and holler, "Is that damn coon in there?" Danny and I would be obliged to leave by the back door as Grandad came in the front.

These realities made me decide to speed up the taming process and turn Wild into a twenty-dollar bill. The only other alternative was to turn him loose. Everybody else in the family was in agreement, including Danny, but Grandad put a question mark to the idea when he said that it was going to be impossible to sell a completely wild coon for anywhere near twenty dollars, as a person would have to be crazy to buy it. He had a point. He had another one, too, when he suggested that there was only one such person in the country and he already had a pet coon.

One time when I was pondering this problem, I mentioned that maybe the next coon I caught would be a female and then I could get into the coon business in a big way. Dad was never able to see the light. He was still promoting the theory that the only jobs or businesses a person should try for were white-collar ones, even though he himself had never had one. His union activity, which was supposed to have led to one, got him blacklisted, so now he was having to raise rabbits and carve totem poles for a lot less than coons could be sold for. Why are there so many dilemmas in this world and why is it that most of them lead to some type of brink? Rusty, Danny, and I went back to the river for a day to think this thing out and sure enough, while waiting for a fish to bite, the answer descended.

In those times there was in New Westminster a place called the "Farmers Market," where we could buy or sell anything that was raised on the local land. We often bought things there and even sold some of our rabbits through it, though so far I had never seen a raccoon in there. There is a first time for everything and I was becoming aware that firsts seemed to be my preference. This Farmers Market seemed to have possibilities. I'd put down fifty cents for a stall and come out with a twenty-dollar sale, and I'd build on Don Grant's recent salesmanship lesson about buying a "half tame" coon "as is, where is." Instead of taking a coon into the Market in a sack, I would build a small wire-mesh cage and sell coon and cage as a single unit. When Don sold me a coon, he explicitly advised me not to let the upset coon out of the sack and not to expect it to act too domesticated for a few days. This had to be the answer.

When I arrived home with both a good-sized fish and the new business plan, it was again Dad who tried dampening it down. His theory was there was a difference between Don Grant's sales pitch to me, when he knew in his own mind that Danny really was about half tame, and my plan to sell a coon as half tame when I knew he was more like 98 percent wild. When I tried quizzing him about how anybody could prove the difference, he became frustrated and kept using a word that I did not understand the meaning of, but if memory serves me right it sounded something like "fraud." I could not see how looking up the meaning in the dictionary would improve the sales potential, so I didn't bother to do it. Dad and I argued about that through three suppers until he finally tossed in the towel by exclaiming "Oh, Jesus Christ" and ended the discussion by getting up to go into the front room and read the newspaper.

The next project was making the display cage. Considering that all the materials were scrounged, it did not increase my expenses and even looked presentable, especially considering who made it. It then became part of Wild's inside pen and I enticed him into it with sardines. If milk led to Danny's undoing, sardines did the same to Wild. He got so he knew what was in an unopened can, though Dad suggested that he may have learned it from garbage cans up near Langley. Whatever the case, they worked, even though they cost nine cents per can. I made a mental note that this could be a selling point for a city buyer as it was probable that was where his new home would be. Grandad kept harping that the city people weren't as dumb as I was hoping they were and I might end up bringing Wild back home again.

At that time we were operating what was supposed to be the biggest rabbitry in B.C. We butchered 180 rabbits twice a week and delivered them to Woodward Stores and Blackburn Market in Vancouver, so on one of those delivery days, a Saturday morning, I hitched a ride with Dad as far as Farmers Market in New Westminster. He would pick me up there on his return, probably, as he said several times, "still packing that damn raccoon around."

Well did he and Grandad ever have it all wrong. Just as soon as Wild and I entered the building we had an appreciative audience trailing us. Within minutes after I arranged for a booth and set the cage up on the table, it was the most popular place in the market. Wild was in good form and remained in a puffed-up condition for long periods of time, never backing away from anybody. He spent his day daring everybody to put a finger through that wire, and the fools who tried soon learned who owned the cage. The standard question I had to keep answering was, "Just how tame is that raccoon?" To calm all fears, I repeated over and over again that he was only acting this way because he was upset from the car ride and he was not used to crowds. As soon as someone took him home to a quiet place, he would settle down again. I actually believed the pitch to be true, but at the same time tried to stay within sight of Dad's guidelines, which I interpreted as "Don't tell a complete lie and don't volunteer the type of information that can be turned around and brought back to roost again."

One woman wanted to know if Wild was trained to a leash yet and I told her the truth, which was, "No he isn't. I never thought to try him on one. But coons are real smart and I'm sure that with a little time and patience, he will learn fast." I forgot to mention that Wild had not yet had a human hand laid on him, but the woman was just curious and not a buyer type.

Then there came one of those pretty little Dutch girls that the area abounded with. She was very impressed with Wild and seemed maybe the same with me, so I gave her the royal treatment. I taught her how to purr to Wild. Within a few minutes he was talking back to her and she was much taken by him, but she had no money and all I got out of it was some stimulating thoughts and conversation.

The exhibition went on for a couple of hours until a small group was passing by and a young, good-looking woman stopped dead in her tracks as she exclaimed, "Oh, isn't he cute!"

Those words were a bell-ringer as I instantly sensed, "If she has twenty dollars, Wild has a new owner."

The woman came right over and squatted in front of the cage with her nose just out of Wild's reach and asked me, "What's his name?"

I had already taken note that several other people seemed to think Wild's name and his actions were related, so this time I decided on a different tack and the coon underwent an instant name change. "His name is Daniel Coon, but I call him Danny."

"Oh isn't that a cute name for him," she agreed. "I'll bet that's a pun on Daniel Boone, isn't it?"

I didn't know what the word "pun" meant, but the woman was coming across like she might be about half smart, so rather than expose myself I just smiled and nodded and hoped for the best. Wild seemed to be taking to her well, so I taught her how to talk to a raccoon and the coon quickly replied. Those two were coming together fast, so I laid on everything within the legal limits.

During the conversation she asked me what seemed like an out-of-place question. "Where do you go to school?"

"Out at White Rock," I answered.

"Oh, that's interesting," she replied. "Last year I almost went to work out there."

The conversation was becoming more friendly and personal, so to keep it going I asked her, "Working at what?"

"Oh, didn't I mention it? I'm a schoolteacher," she replied.

I hoped it didn't show on my face or in my eyes, but my mental reaction to those words would not have been much different if she said she was a truant officer, a Gestapo agent, or with the NKVD. Even though she was pretty and seemed interesting, she had just admitted to being one of "Them."

She was still crouched there, bubbling away with the coon, when she turned to me and asked, "How much do you want for Danny Coon?"

Without the slightest hesitation or qualm I answered, "Twenty-five dollars."

"Oh, that's a lot of money," she smiled back.

I had seen teachers smile before and it seldom did any of us any good, so I wasn't about to be taken in this time either. "Yeah, it is, but I've put a lot of work into this coon and I know he has great possibilities of becoming a great pet and friend for the right type of person." Then just to thicken the bait a bit more I told her all about my other raccoon whose name was Wild and who would follow me all over the yard and even sleep in my bed when Mom wasn't looking.

"Oh, that's just exactly the kind of raccoon I want," the teacher exclaimed, but she apparently needed a little more convincing as she asked, "Do you think that Danny Coon would learn to live in an apartment building?"

"Oh, I'm sure he will do just fine," I advised her and then went into detail about how easy it had been to teach the coons to adapt to their change of homes in Surrey.

It must have been a convincing discussion because her next statement was, "Okay, I'll buy Danny Coon from you, and I sure hope he will learn to do all the things you say he will."

"Oh, he sure will," I assured her. "All it takes is time and kindness and he will do all that and then some." Then to seal the deal on friendly and truthful instructions, I passed on Don Grant's theory that it would be a good idea not to turn the coon loose too soon, but wait a few days until she knew she could trust it. "If I was you, I'd wait until you know that you and the coon have nice warm thoughts for each other," was my final recommendation.

When she opened her purse to pay me, she handed over two tens and a five, and I noticed that she had much more in there. I mentally chastised myself for not asking forty dollars. I had not realized that schoolteachers were so overpaid, but a deal is a deal. I gallantly picked up the caged coon and carried it out to the car for her. Her parting remarks were, "I can hardly wait to be able to let Danny Coon out of that small cage so I can begin training him. I know that we are going to have exciting times together."

Rather than take a chance of spoiling things with words, I just smiled, nodded in agreement, and waved good-bye. Other than being one of "Them," the woman seemed like she could have been a nice person.

When Dad came to pick me up, his first words were, "Where is the raccoon?"

"Sold him in less than an hour."

He gave me an almost incredulous look as he asked, "How much did you get for him?"

"Twenty-five bucks," was my bravado reply as I waved two tens at him and nodded to the small package on the car seat that contained ten boxes of .22 short cartridges that had cost a total of $3.80, leaving enough to buy a beef sandwich for lunch with the change.

His next question was, "Did you tell the buyer that the coon was still completely wild?"

"That coon is not completely wild as he is eating just fine, so that means he is almost half tame. And anyway," I laughed, "the woman said she is a schoolteacher and knows all about training wild things, so she shouldn't have too many problems with this one."

Dad's reply as he jumped the car into gear was, "You damn young shyster, some day these things are all going to catch up to you."

Now that the venture had proven to be interesting and profitable, I immediately went upriver with another chicken and reset the trap. It took close to a month before I caught another coon, and over the two-year period I was able to catch only five of them. There were two reasons for this I could think of. The first, mentioned earlier, was that there was a shortage of raccoons in Surrey. As well, coons tend to hunt in pairs and even entire families, so when one was caught it warned the others, and these must have been smart enough to equate bush cages with chickens in them with danger. I never was able to locate a lady coon for Danny, so there was never a chance to try the "born in captivity" bit, which would certainly have been easier than the wild way.

The following four coons were sold under the exact same circumstances as Wild was. They went to Market as soon as they were feeding well and the look and acts of panic had worn off, which usually took about a week. No other buyers identified themselves as schoolteachers, so the other four were sold for the going rate of twenty dollars each.

Dad never did come to full agreement with my salesmanship and he made me agree that if a disgruntled coon buyer asked for the money back, I had to be prepared to issue it. Fortunately this term of sale was never needed, and I never told Dad what was floating in my shadow mind, which was if any spoilsport did ask for a refund, then I would ask for the return of the coon. I figured if anybody could keep a coon long enough to locate me, by that time it really would be half tame and could be legally resold as such. To deal with the chance that someone might want to come and discuss such an issue, I signed for my stalls and introduced myself as Ed Duncan, which being my first and middle names, did not make a lie either.

The memories of those "as is, where is" deals have often haunted my mind. Not the morality part because being at least half legal, they were all part of life's game. The question that still squirms in the shadow is what happened to the five coons and to the people who bought them? Every one of those buyers was a young woman, and I do hope that all of those women enjoyed their rascally little coons as much as I did mine.

CHAPTER 10

GOOD-BYE

Some people see time as a condition of being unable to prevent the sand from running out, but in my early life I saw it as just the opposite. By the time I was fifteen going on sixteen, I was very much aware that I was not like my friends of the same age group or even the older ones, because I never suffered from the dilemma others complained about of being "bored shitless" as the expression was. They said it was because there was nothing interesting to do. The truth was, those fools were blind. For those of us who were then passing into young adulthood, everything was going on.

World War Two was recently over and by 1948 we were surrounded by the people who had been part of it—on both sides. There were boatloads of Germans arriving in Canada. In the Lower Mainland of B.C. it was more Dutchmen, and then on top of that, all of our own boys were returning home too, and they all had stories to tell. There were also a few who wanted to forget everything they knew about the recent history, but hardly anybody wanted to listen to them. And for all of those who wanted to try it again, especially the young hot bloods who had missed out on the previous engagement, the politicians and officer corps puffed up the pipes and rattled the drums and by 1950 we were out for blood and glory again. The Korean War was in full force. As adults had told us as far back as anybody could remember, there would always be another war. For any boy that figured he missed the excitement of plugging a Kraut or a Jap, they now offered us legal targets that were portrayed in the media as Gooks. You may not like the sound of those words today, but fifty and fewer years ago our generation grew up on them. It was called propaganda, but we went for it anyway, hook, line, and sinker.

Not all the boys were duped by the war frenzy, as there was another smaller group that stayed home and created its own excitement. During those late 1940s and early 1950s there was a huge surge of bank robberies. Quite a few of the Robin Hoods were never caught, which was an inducement for others to try. The way the media played them up some weeks, it was like reading the sports pages. Those boys were popular and it was easy for the rest of us to relate to them. For one thing, how many people love a bank? In many people's minds, banks were considered to be fair game.

For certain types of people, opportunity and temptations abounded and all it took was a clear eye, a steady hand, and the world could be your oyster. Potential rewards could be seen everywhere. Glory with one and money with the other. For the winners, women came with both.

Those temptations didn't hook everybody, and there was another group that preferred the land right here to a grave in a far-off land or the fifty-fifty chance of rotting the rest of our lives out in a jail. To begin with, several young friends and I worked the local farms. Then I graduated from them to the boats on the lower Fraser River, spending one summer on a co-op fish collector, the *Nabob*, out of Whonnock and owned by Anchor Gilstead, and my last summer there on a beachcomber tug, *Weaver Lake*, owned by Charlie Merchant out of Mission City. Those were interesting summers too, but what they taught me most was neither of them was the life of adventure or anything close to it. Speaking of dull boredom, have you ever read Karl Marx, Engels, Lenin, or Stalin? Well the summer on the *Nabob* finished me off on those lines of thought as Anchor Gilstead was an avowed Communist and a very evangelical one too. He was out to redden the world, but the season I spent with him he convinced more clients and crew that he was preaching a dead-end line then he ever converted to his faith. The summer as a beachcomber with Charlie Merchant was far more interesting as Charlie's philosophy was about the opposite of Anchor's, something like "Rules and laws are made to be broken." It sounded like he was good at it too, and as far as I know he never spent a day in jail. Charlie's stories could beat the hell out of Marx or bloody-minded Joe Stalin any day of the week. He was also an avid hunter and fisherman and was related to many of the same up and down the Fraser, so we shared many views about things and that does make for easy work relationships.

The work on the tug had its exciting moments if you consider danger exciting. For instance, we were into the boom-towing business mostly, at least in the daylight hours, and what that meant was loosening the log booms from the shore pilings, setting them free in mid-river, sorting them, and then connecting them for the tow to the mills downstream. Above Mission City the Fraser is a mighty strong river, and walking those boom sticks is tricky business. Us deck hands had to be fast on our feet and good swimmers if we weren't. In 1951, when I did my stint at it, we were not allowed to wear caulked boots on the boat, and the only life preservers on it were two of those cork rings that lifeguards throw at people. I don't remember either of ours ever being taken off the rack. It was about the same on the other boats too, and every year at least a couple of deck hands went under. Those boomsticks were slippery. I do not remember one that was not wet and slick as snot, and we seemed to work with the worst ones at night. When we accidentally looked into the glare of the searchlight, it almost always resulted in a splash and then a mad scramble to get back up on a log again before the boom closed over us. There were such near-death experiences almost daily and stories of the kids who never surfaced fast enough. By the time the invisible films of November ice on the logs began adding to the fun, I decided to leave the glory to the rest and bid the lower Fraser River and Charlie Merchant good-bye.

I went home for a while to cast around and began mulling over thoughts like joining the army or the RCMP and going to the Yukon, but I was still too young for either. Always in the back of my mind were thoughts of the stories the Haslers had told of the north country, and they were strong enough to still need checking out. Tom Hasler had sold his Elgin farm to the Wickland family in about 1947 or 1948 and moved away, and I only saw him one more time after that. The Wicklands built the Covered Wagon Auto Court on some of the land and farmed the rest of it. They all became friends too, but they were nothing like the Hasler boys, as a person only has an experience like them once in a lifetime. I fully appreciated my time with them and still have fondest memories to today.

It turned out to be my other best friend, Don Turnbull, who set my life on its next course. He invited me to accompany him on a moose-hunting expedition to some place "up country" that he called the Chilcotin. The Cariboo was a household word in B.C., but the Chilcotin was not, probably because one had gold and the other didn't.

The place we were heading for was another unknown called Alexis Creek, where Don's brother Bob was the lone RCMP member for the entire Chilcotin district. Somewhere out beyond Alexis Creek the Turnbulls had a family friend named Jack Maindley who had a small cattle ranch and was also a part-time hunting guide. The major reason Don invited me on this excursion was Stu MacBeth, who was scheduled to go, could not make it at the last minute and Don wanted somebody to go along and share the expenses and road experiences. It came together at a good time as I had bought a second-hand model 94 Winchester 30:30 from Don and also had $800 from tugboating that was burning a hole in my pocket. At the time, after looking over Don's maps of the area, I knew this was not the real north country, but it was certainly north of where we were so just for the experience I asked, "When do we leave?"

"Day after tomorrow," Don replied. And by God, we did.

It was early November 1951 when Don and I headed north in his 1935 three-ton Maple Leaf truck. It had a suspension system that rode like a covered wagon, but it took us through the Cariboo and into the Chilcotin, though not without travel events. I still remember how the pavement of the Cariboo highway ended rather abruptly when we passed through Lac La Hache. It was dark when we arrived at the spot and there was no warning sign or marker that at the end of the pavement there was a two-foot-deep hole, an indication of the condition the old Cariboo Road was famous for. Have you ever hit a two-foot-deep hole in the dark in a 1935 Maple Leaf truck going forty miles per hour? If you have, then you'll know what I'm talking about because all the same things happened to us too. The headlights that were mounted on the front crossbar fell off, so did the muffler, and a strange new sound came out of the transmission. It is annoying to have things like that happen in strange country and in the dark. One of the headlights was broken, so we tossed it into the back of the truck and Don spliced some wire together so we could tape and clamp the other one to the hood, and that's how we slowly drove into Williams Lake in the middle of the night. It was a cold night too, but Don laughed it off and warned me to start getting used to it because it could drop to sixty below just any time it felt like it. Sounded interesting.

Daylight the next morning revealed Williams Lake was not much of a town, probably not as big as Cloverdale, but we were able to locate a bulb for the broken headlight. A little more wiring and we had a strange headlight system, but in daylight we could travel without them. From then on the lights were only for emergency use, and as the transmission was no noisier than before, we headed westward. The muffler wasn't fixed either, so we travelled with our heads out the window—and when we left Williams Lake, the temperature was reading out at fifteen below Fahrenheit. Don said the road would become worse the further we went, and he sure never exaggerated on that point. I had about as tough a body as any sixteen year old could have, but when we arrived at Alexis Creek a few hours later, that bruised body was about ready to admit defeat.

That night we stayed with and visited Don's brother Bob, his wife Rose, and their big Lassie-type collie whose name was Ace. Bob was the first Mountie I had ever met and Ace was about the most spoiled dog. Ace seemed to be the centre of the family and he knew it and used his position to considerable advantage in the name of self-interest. As for the Mountie, Bob Turnbull was nothing like what I was hoping he would be. I was expecting to meet the full red serge outfit, but he didn't even wear a uniform or a pistol. He did have a badge of some sort clipped to his belt where it couldn't be seen. This Mountie wore a Cowichan Indian sweater and a regular western-style hat. I'd never been away from the Lower Mainland before, where all cops wore full uniform with one and sometimes two pistols, so I was curious and asked Bob about the difference. He explained that this was usually a very dusty country and he was often still having to patrol on horseback, so keeping a uniform clean to RCMP standards was hardly possible. He had it figured that regular outdoor clothing was much more practical, and he didn't need the uniform for identification as everybody in the country knew who and what he was anyway. He was convincing as it all made sense to someone like me.

Later that same evening I commented to Bob that this day had shown me, with the exception of the road, what I considered to be the most beautiful country I had ever seen. He laughed as he told me, "You had better like this country, because the road you are going over tomorrow is still pretty well a wagon road and that old truck might not make it back out of there. You might end up having to learn to ride a horse and come out on the green grass of next summer." He intended it as a joke, but his remark turned out to be prophetic.

We got an early start next morning and the twenty-eight-mile trip up onto the Jackpine Plateau of the Chilcotin, where Jack Maindley had his ranch, took us several hours as the road turned out to be everything Bob said it was going to be. We managed to get stuck in the mud twice and the headlights both fell off again, so we left them stored on the seat and didn't try remounting them until the truck returned to conventional roads again. When we arrived at the ranch we were met by Don's father Bill and his friend Harvey Boone who were there moose hunting, and of course by Jack Maindley, who turned out to be in his late sixties. As Don and I intended to stay for two weeks, one of the first things Don did was offer my services to Jack for a few days. He said this was to help me adjust to my new surroundings. There was no problem with that as Old Jack (as he was known to all) and I hit it off real well together. For the next few days I followed him around and helped batten down the ranch for the coming winter, fixing some holes in the rail fences, cutting a bigger supply of wood and using the three-ton to haul it in with, tightening up sagging gates, and things like that. Most of those jobs were little different from what I had grown up doing. It looked to me like the only part of working a ranch I was totally unfamiliar with was riding a horse. The only time I had ever been on one was at the Tara Riding Stable, where we paid fifty cents an hour to bruise our butts. My opinion of horses was there had to be better ways to spend hard-earned money. When I mentioned that to Jack he just laughed and told me, "When your ass gets sore enough, you'll learn to ride properly."

For the following two weeks our routine was hunting in the mornings and ranch chores in the afternoons. Moose hunting that fall was not easy as there were three inches of crusted snow that made stalking them difficult. There were lots of moose around the ranch, but because of that snow condition only Harvey and I got a bull apiece. Mine was a huge old animal that must have been going dotty because for no reason he ran right up to within fifty yards of me and he and I initiated each other. He turned out to be the biggest moose I have ever killed, and his meat was so tough that I never want to try an older one.

The last few days on the ranch were spent mostly on the woodpile, which did not seem to give off the same negative feelings as the one at home did. I just kept volunteering for more work. Even in my own mind I knew there must be something wrong with me because this was nowhere near normal. The new feeling was turning out to be something like not wanting to leave.

The saws we were using were the crosscut types and they were so dull that they could only make fine sawdust, but one afternoon Harvey remembered he had a couple of files in his jeep. Apparently Old Jack had never learned to file a saw, even though his axes were sharp enough, but it was something Dad had taught me how to do. Don had learned it somewhere too, perhaps from his father, and when we finished working Jack's two saws over, they were back to pulling out one-inch shavings and we really did make the chips fly. About then Jack happened to walk by and stopped to watch our progress and he made a comment that set my mind to wondering. What he said was, "By God, boy, you could become a handy person to have around a place like this."

For the rest of the day I contemplated that statement because on my arrival back home I had no particular job to go to and I needed one. As of three months earlier, school had become past history for my life. For the coming spring I had planned to head out on a tuna boat that had been bringing in fabulous catches not far from the B.C. coast. It was a new industry then. My long-range plans were still to head up into the Tom Hasler country and buy a trapline, but I needed a money stake first and probably experience in open country. Thoughts like these kept piling up in my mind.

Add to them the fact that Jack had mentioned several times his problems keeping a hired hand on this remote location. At that time there was no hired hand on the ranch, but Jack had made contact with one who was due to arrive soon, and he was watching the gate for his arrival. He needed help, as he was badly crippled from arthritis.

The thoughts kept spinning along and even though the idea of becoming a ranch hand or cowboy had never crossed my mind before, it was beginning to have an appeal, with the only stumbling block being I was leery of using horses. I knew absolutely nothing about them, but everything on this ranch and most of the others in the vicinity centred on them. Jack had bought his first tractor just the year before, and he still did not own a truck. He made it sound like Chilcotin and horses were synonymous words. He had lived a long lifetime with horses, and his stories could whet a person's curiosity. I was young, impressionable, and turning eager, so one evening I made the plunge and hit him up for a job. We were all at the table at the time so it became a group decision. Don, Harvey, and Bill all conceded that it would be a great experience and as Bill suggested, "Every kid should put in a year or two on a ranch or farm, just to settle him down before going on to more serious occupations."

Jack was sort of in agreement too, but there was the problem of the expected new hand, whose name was Dave. Until Dave left, no job was available, but Jack said he would sure get word to me in a hurry if and when Dave gave it up. So that's the way we left it.

Don figured it was the best way to do it and said I should go back to the coast first, if for no other reason than to say good-bye to my friends and folks. He also was having qualms about how well the truck was going to behave and if something did go wrong, two sets of hands were better than one. Just to be the spoilsport he sometimes was, he also suggested that when we returned to Surrey I should consider going back to school. I believe that he was one of those people who enjoy making other people go through the same suffering he did, something like "misery loves company." But I had already mentally burned that bridge, so he could suffer it out alone or maybe con his own kids into it. This kid was too smart to finish school.

The trip out was a bit eventful, even though we had an 800-pound moose and a ton of wood for ballast, which sure helped. They were no asset when the brakes gave out going down the hill towards Alexandria Bridge. Don was a good driver and was able to bring the truck to a safe stop, but we then learned that the hydraulic pump was not fixable. We started out again and Don was doing just fine at shifting through a lot of gears that kept us in control until he waited too long for a shift going down a hill just north of Hope in the Fraser Canyon. The engine was winding up and getting hot enough that we could smell burning oil over top of the exhaust fumes. Then Don hollered at me to get ready to jump, so I opened the door and had my feet on the running board, ready to do it. Everything was noise and smoke and all of a sudden there was more noise that sounded like the engine was thinking of coming back into the cab with us. I heard Don scream, “I think we just blew a rod!” The speedometer read something over sixty and I was trying to spot out a soft-looking landing spot but luckily never mustered up the nerve to try for one. And also luckily, Don was able to bring the truck to a red-hot stop.

After letting it cool off and then restarting it, Don confirmed that, yes, we had a broken piston rod. The engine still ran okay but noisily, so we limped into Hope at five miles per hour. Maple Leaf trucks were never popular and there was no hope of getting parts in Hope, so Don, being a good bush mechanic, took the pan off and disconnected the broken rod, then lifted the piston in place. In 1951, Hope was not a very big place, so every man in town ventured by to watch and comment on our work. Some said it would work and some said we would never get out of town, but it did work. One old guy offered to drive us and the loose gear home for half the moose meat. I thought it was a pretty good idea, especially if it was Don’s half. After all, it was his truck that was letting us down, piece by piece. But he was the boss of our outfit and did not consider it to be a good deal, so we started out on the last seventy-five-mile leg of our odyssey with no brakes and one cylinder short, and by God we made it home without having to stop once.

After that I did odd jobs on the local farms and got my confirmation of a berth to the tuna water for the following spring, so things were still looking pretty good for me. One good season with the tuna would make a stake for the north country.

A message at Christmas changed all those plans. Old Jack sent down word that the isolation of the ranch was getting to the new hired hand and Dave wanted out. So there was a dilemma over whether to wait for the fortunes in the tuna water or head up into the Chilcotin sticks in midwinter.

When I informed Mom and Dad of my decision, they were absolutely dumbfounded. Dad's argument was the cowboy and hunting life had died out at the turn of the century and you cannot hold back progress. My guess was based on pure hope, as I argued back that it would last at least one more lifetime, namely mine. Mom said if I went to Chilcotin for the wages it paid, I would never be able to afford to come back and visit my friends again and they would scatter to the wind with better jobs than I was going to. So some are right and some are wrong. We all live our own lives.

It was January 4, 1952, when I climbed into the Greyhound bus in New Westminster and headed up the Cariboo Road towards whatever fate and future had in store for me. I can still remember the trip and the feeling that came over me as the bus travelled out over the Pattullo Bridge that day. Looking down onto the lower Fraser River, the city of New Westminster sliding behind, my shadow mind bid them good-bye. "Good-bye you swarms of people, good-bye cities, good-bye salt-chuck and all that goes with you."

And the real finale arrived up at the ranch later that year in the form of a newspaper article informing the world that for some unknown reason the tuna had failed to come within fishing distance of B.C. I do not believe they ever returned again.

PIONEER VOICES

A Word About the Heritage House Pioneer Voices Series

Western Doctor's Odyssey. This is the story of Eldon Lee's formative years and his first practice in Hazelton, BC. In an era of corporate medicine and malpractice insurance, Dr. Lee's story is a refreshing reminder of what doctoring is all about. ($11.95)

Tall in the Saddle by Eldon and Todd Lee finds two brothers sharing their recollections and observations about growing up on the Hill and Paul Ranch in the Cariboo region of British Columbia. ($14.95)

Totem Poles and Tea by Hughina Harold has been called "an adult version of Anne of Green Gables" and a "must-read for all BCers" by independent reviewers. It is an enlightening story of a young nurse-teacher's corning of age in a remote 1930s native village. ($17.95)

Chilcotin: Preserving Pioneer Memories by the Witte Sisters. Vivid text and over 200 photographs recall country extending some 200 miles west from the Fraser River to Anahim Lake ($39.95)

Looking Back at the Cariboo-Chilcotin with Irene Stangoe. Irene's second books is a new collection of heritage stories set in the Cariboo-Chilcotin. Blending fact, legend and local hearsay, Irene entertains and educates in a folksy down-home voice that has won her wide acclaim.

THE AUTHOR

Ed Choate was born into the Great Depression in southwestern British Columbia in 1935. Living next to the Nicomekl River, his youth was a series of adventures that conjure up mixed images of Huck Finn, Billy the Kid, and a young Davy Crockett.

Caring parents, a loving home, the ethics-challenged Hasler brothers, and a teacher or two helped steer him through some pitfalls until he left home at sixteen to spend a life next to nature.

Chilco tried his hand at cowboyin' but quickly gravitated to the life of a big game guide and outfitter. The day he bought his guide lease he had 32 healthy teeth pulled in one sitting and replaced with "choppers" because he never wanted to fall victim to a toothache back in the bush where his customer's lives depended on him. Soon home was beside Lake Gaspard on the Chilcotin Plateau in central B.C. (about 51°20' latitude, 123° longitude). He quickly became known as Chilco Choate, a handle that stuck.

In later years Chilco became an active and well-known conservationist, a strong advocate of "more green and less people."

If Chilco has mellowed over the years, it is hard to notice. He is stone deaf, probably from being in the neighbourhood of too much gunfire. Friend John Taylor once wrote "There isn't a newspaper publisher, bureaucrat, or politician who hasn't been held accountable by the inexhaustible stream of Choate letters that flow through the Riske Creek post office. His grammar is rough and his spelling imaginative, but there's nothing wrong with his storytelling. He's outwitted, outwritten, and, outlived most of his enemies. He's one of a kind, the last of his kind, and you'll find it all in a book he was born to write."

Chilco's first book, *Unfriendly Neighbours,* depicted his running battle and volatile relationship with the Gang Ranch. His next book for Heritage will recall his many adventures over four decades as outfitter, hunting guide, conservationist, and provocateur in the Gang Ranch country of the Chilcotin.